Compassionate Artificial Intelligence

Compassionate Artificial Intelligence

Amit Ray, PhD

Founder Compassionate AI Lab

Compassionate AI Lab
www.compassionateailab.com

Published

by

COMPASSIONATE AI LAB

First Published 2018

ISBN: 978-938212346-0

Email: info@compassionateailab.com

www.compassionateailab.com

Contents

Preface

I had two main objectives in writing this book. One is to explore the possibility of designing comprehensive intelligent systems that can learn, adapt and compassionately serve human needs. The second is to develop intelligent systems that can understand and prevent evil actions and commands by wrongly motivated forces.

In this book, I have addressed those issues and explained the concept of Compassionate Artificial Intelligence (CAI), which integrates the algorithm of compassionate thinking that not only makes a system prevent an action designed by corrupted or wrongly motivated commands, but also makes a system sensitive to the human needs of pain, loneliness and suffering.

It may sound like a little tall order right now to make a machine compassionate to human needs, but it is worth striving for developing a comprehensive and safe system for the benefit of humanity. In this book, I explain how the emerging technologies like Internet of things (IoT), Quantum computing, Cellular reprogramming and genome editing, Drone, Computer Aided Drug Design, Brain-Computer-Interface, Blockchain, Big data can be used with deep learning and other modern artificial intelligence (AI) architectures for the ultimate level of evolution of machine intelligence. The remarkable progress in AI research in the last few years, encourage us to believe that such comprehensive compassionate intelligent system is indeed possible to develop that will have the ability to think, learn, imagine and become self-aware.

I call it Compassionate Artificial Intelligence, which empowers machine with compassion along with intelligence, creativity, connectivity, and which will help the humanity and machine to jointly evolve and reach new levels of consciousness. Such compassionate intelligent systems would be a boon to the human society rather than being an evil force.

The real challenge is how to digitize and incorporate the human values like compassion, forgiveness, bravery, morality, love and creativity in AI based systems. In this book, I explored compassionate artificial intelligence in depth. The book provides the blueprint, directions, frameworks, algorithms, principles and strategies to develop such compassionate artificial intelligent systems in the coming days.

In writing the book, I acknowledge my gratitude to the students, researchers and the volunteers of Compassionate AI Lab, who persistently insisted me and finally convinced me to write this book.

Finally, this book would not have been possible without the encouragement, help and support of my wife Banani. I am deeply indebted to her for her precious analytical comments, criticism and suggestions at every step of writing this book.

Dr. Amit Ray
25th September, 2018

Introduction

In the last five years there has been an exponential growth in the development of artificial intelligent (AI) systems. The gap between human and artificial intelligent systems are reducing exponentially. With the advancement of AI, autonomous weapon system, and nuclear war technology, gradually mankind is moving towards a great danger.

Also there is a genuine threat from the AI systems itself. The exponential growth of intelligence in AI systems poses a real threat that one day the AI systems will surpass humans in every aspect. With the rapid development of new technologies, and given the much greater ability of the machines to hold, analyze and process the huge database, which is mounting up through the use of gadgets like the smart phones and medical Apps, the limited human brains will fall far short of the machines. Moreover, humans have their limitations of hunger, thirst, old age, disease and emotional setbacks.

Hence, the question is whether humans will use AI systems or will end up being used by them. Will humans be at the mercy of the machines in not so far future? Will the machines treat humans like pets? There is all probability that it can happen. Many scientists and experts believe that with the growing development of AI technology, the future of humanity is facing the bleak existential threat from the killer robots and immortal dictators.

Admitting the validity of their apprehension, I would like to believe in the other extreme of the possibility, which is the potential to use the AI systems for the benefit of the humankind and the world in much deeper sense.

Compassionate artificial intelligence is the way to come out of the threat posed by the machines, which can be made more responsible, more efficient, more intelligent and more adaptable than the mortal humans with limited capacities. Designing compassionate AI based systems is an urgent need today.

Compassionate artificial intelligence systems are also required for looking after those unable to care for themselves, especially sick, physically challenged persons, children or elderly people.

Modern research needs to move in the direction of compassionate AI systems that should provide empathetic listening, intelligent decisions, warm touch, beautiful and encouraging words, and soft and loving voice with faithful services. They should understand human safety, freedom, emotions, moods and feelings with patience. They should also provide soft intellectual and creative arguments and funs to uplift human moods and boost the human spirit.

Compassionate AI system should also have important roles to play in eliminating terrorism, human pain and mass destruction. Compassionate AI based honey-bee style drones can be used for disaster management and emergency services.

However, the first thing we need to understand is that compassionate AI system is not like a servant-robot. The intelligence of a compassionate AI system can be a non-local, non-hierarchical distributed network which is based on highest human ethics and values. We should realize that compassionate AI system is neither a servant, nor a toy that can be manipulated by individual will. Speaking about the compassionate AI system, it will be a distributed, decentralized, and democratized intelligence that can access the collective intelligence and will have brain-to-computer and computer-to brain communication skills.

The challenge is how to design compassionate artificial intelligent systems, which has the capacity of deep compassion, deep learning, and deep brain-to-brain connectivity. This is particularly possible with the advancement of quantum computing, AI and other technological breakthroughs.

I have three main aims in writing this book. The first is to explain the need and urgency to develop the compassionate AI systems in today's world threatened with nuclear warfare, terrorism, corruption, rogue states and monster governments.

The second aim is to show how emerging technologies like Internet of things (IoT), Quantum computing, Cellular reprogramming and genome editing, Drone, Brain-Computer-Interface, Blockchain, Big data can be used with deep learning, reinforcement learning and other modern artificial intelligence (AI) architectures for the ultimate level of machine intelligence. The third aim is to propose compassionate AI design and behavioral principles and algorithms that can be easily implemented.

A clear and simple account of the key ideas, principles and algorithms of compassionate AI are discussed. I have also covered the current developments in AI and related topics, which will guide you through the major topics covered in the book. To adequately address these three aims, some conceptual clarifications are necessary. To this end, I have explored the concepts of agents and AI agents. I have introduced the concepts of compassionate AI agents and compassionate superintelligence that can be a blessing for the humanity and all beings in the world.

Chapter - 1

The Need for Compassionate AI

Since compassionate artificial intelligence (CAI) aims to emulate properties of biological compassion systems, it is appropriate to start the discussion with the biological dimension of compassion. Biological compassion strongly suggest that it is necessary to consider a CAI system be sensitive towards the environment it inhabits and interacts with.

In this chapter first we will discuss the biological, physical, and behavioral properties of compassion in the light of current research. Then we will discuss the need for compassionate artificial intelligence.

What is compassion?

Compassion is considered as a faculty of higher consciousness. We all feel compassion when we see our family or friends in distress, and even animals feel compassion when they see their offspring are in pain. Compassion is a form of emotional engagement that is benevolent to the sufferer and the humanity.

Compassion involves the sharing of feelings of another as a means of coming to an understanding and appreciation for how they feel. Hence, compassion is the feelings, inner experiences and related efforts to remove the pain of others. Compassion is an inbuilt human nature. It is the human potential to reach the higher evolution of consciousness. Compassion comprises of feelings, emotions, sentiment and understanding.

Formal Definitions of Compassion

Compassion is the feeling that arises in witnessing another's suffering and that motivates a subsequent desire to help (Goetz, Keltner, & Simon-Thomas, 2010). We would place the states labeled with terms like “sympathy,” “empathy” and “pity,” into a family of compassion-related states that center upon a concern for improving the suffering of another individual or groups.

Kanov et al., (2004), says that compassion consists of three facets: noticing, feeling, and responding. ‘Noticing’ includes being aware of a person's suffering, either by cognitively recognizing this suffering or by experiencing an unconscious physical or affective reaction to it. 'Feeling' is defined as responding emotionally to that suffering and experiencing 'empathic concern' through accepting the person's perspective and imagining or feeling their condition. Finally, 'responding' encompasses having a desire to act to alleviate the person's suffering.

From the empathic distress perspective, compassion is simply a label that people apply to their indirect experience of distress in response to another person's suffering. The clear implication is that the state of compassion should be associated with the expressive behavior, physiological response, and underlying appraisals of the state it is mirroring, most likely distress, pain, sadness, or fear (Goetz et al., 2010). Hence, compassion can be defined as the altruistic concern for another person's suffering and the desire or motivation to alleviate it (Nussbaum, 1996). Gilbert (2010) proposes compassion as consisting of six 'attributes': sensitivity, sympathy, empathy, motivation/caring, distress tolerance and non-judgement. 'Sensitivity' involves being responsive to other people's emotions and perceiving when they need help. The final two components in Gilbert's (2010) model of compassion —'distress tolerance' and 'non-judgement'— are very important. Strauss et al. (2016) propose a new definition of compassion as a cognitive, affective, and behavioral process consisting of the following five elements that refer to both self-compassion and other-compassion: 1) Recognizing suffering; 2) Understanding the universality of suffering in human experience; 3) Feeling empathy for the person suffering, and connecting with the distress (emotional resonance); 4)Tolerating uncomfortable feelings aroused in response to the suffering person (e.g. distress, anger, fear), and so remaining open to and accepting of the person suffering; and 5) Motivation to act to alleviate suffering (Strauss et al., 2016).

Compassion and Evolution:

An evolutionary perspective on compassion can be traced to Darwin (1871), who stated that "those communities which included the greatest number of the most sympathetic members would flourish best, and rear the greatest number of offspring" (Strauss et al.,

2016). Compassion for others is a distinct emotion rooted in the evolution of living beings.

Compassion is an altruistic behavior, an umbrella term which also includes sympathy and empathy. Altruism consists of actions made for the benefit of others, even at a loss to oneself, while empathy involves only feeling the suffering of others in an acute sense. Strangely, altruistic behaviors are seen in several species ranging from bats to chimpanzees - species which that do not appear to teach their offspring the rules of "being nice."

Neuroscience of Compassion:

Compassion is associated with the release of neurotransmitters such as oxytocin and dopamine that are involved in the reward system of the brain, which make us feel good. Neuropsychiatric evidence suggests that the medial wall of pre-frontal cortex (PFC) region of the brain contributes importantly to empathic experience. Research suggests that medial PFC (MPFC) area of the brain is involved in empathic experience and consequent compassionate behavior (Rameson, Morelli, & Lieberman, 2012). High empathy individuals show stronger neural responses than low individuals. MPFC region of the brain has also been associated with thinking about those we feel similar or close to us. MPFC is also associated with higher levels of actions like helping others. During emotions MPFC has the ability to exert rapid control over the autonomic nervous system. The trio consisting of the insula (emotion perception), VLPFC (emotion control), and MPFC (emotion evaluation) work together to facilitate empathy, social communication, and conflict resolution (Pavuluri & May, 2015).

Researchers (Longe et al., 2010), (Lutz, Brefczynski-Lewis, Johnstone, & Davidson, 2008) found that self-compassion engages similar brain regions as expressing compassion towards others.

Why compassion towards self and others makes us feel good? Because compassion activates the "pleasures centers" in the brain. Researchers (Stellar, Cohen, Oveis, & Keltner, 2015) found that vagus nerve appears to be intimately tied to experiencing compassion towards other people's suffering. Compassion relaxes the vagus nerve. The vagus nerve is connected to a range of organs, including the heart and gut, and with the brain through its link to inhibitory prefrontal–subcortical circuits. Heart rate variability (HRV) is an important physiological marker for overall health, and the body–mind connection. Results indicate that compassion is linked to HRV.(Kirby, Doty, Petrocchi, & Gilbert, 2017).

Need for Compassionate AI

The field of AI has been around for more than 60 years, and it has had significant impact on the society. Specially, the machine learning and artificial neural networks have been the key contributors to the AI surge in the past few decades, ranging from the search engines and product recommendation engines to systems designed for speech recognition, natural language processing, prescribing precision medicine, fraud detection, image recognition, and countless other tasks that once depended on human skills and judgments.

Artificial Intelligence (AI) can help us in several ways, especially when combined with Big-data, Blockchain,

Internet of Things, BMI, and robotics. AI can make our everyday life more and more comfortable. It can perform difficult, dangerous and boring works. It can help us save lives, cure illness and cope with disasters more successfully.

Admitted that mass scale domestic robots are not yet walking like cats or dogs or doing our daily jobs like shopping, cleaning, cooking, child care or elder care. But AI technologies are rapidly entering in our life in many different ways. Now, we are taking the help of AI everywhere, not even knowing about it. It is heavily active in search engines, social media, chat bots, medical diagnosis and even built right into our smartphones. Now, AI is at the core of Google's search algorithms. Big companies like Apple, Amazon, Facebook, Google, Tesla, IBM, and Microsoft are spending a lot to explore AI applications they regard critical to their futures.

One may question why it is useful to study compassion in machines at all. Compassion is an important part of human intelligence. The main objective of AI is to serve humanity in an intelligent manner. As AI technology is improving, serving humanity on the surface level is not sufficient. AI can serve humanity in much better way and in a much deeper sense. Compassion, kindness and empathy are the components of higher human intelligence and to be true intelligent, artificial intelligence must incorporate them in the system. The scope and benefits of compassionate AI are many. The requirement for compassionate AI are more urgent than ever.

Robots are leaving the realm of the industry and entering into our homes and workplaces. Humans not just interact with information but also with emotions and feelings. Robots are required to be soft and compassionate towards human.

Compassionate artificial intelligence systems are required for looking after those unable to care for themselves, especially sick, physically challenged persons, children or elderly people. They are required for healthcare, education and for removing the loneliness of people.

Compassionate artificial intelligence systems are also required to stop mass destruction weapon systems. The rapid decision-making capabilities of AI systems are now used for launching nuclear weapons in ships and submarines, especially for preventing counterattacks. AI is also used to control non-nuclear weapons including unmanned vehicles like drones and cyber-weapons. In this competitive age, it is almost certain, that if some-country or someone turn AI into a full-fledged automated weapon system, everyone else will do that too. Initially, it may be just for their own defense but subsequently that will be used for mass destruction. The purpose of compassionate artificial intelligence systems is to develop inbuilt system that can stop and disobey the instructions of evil forces. That evil force can be a machine, an algorithm or a human.

Now, the question is how it is possible to integrate compassion into machines. Scientists argue that if the brain is merely a biological machine, there is no theoretical reason why it could not be replicated, or even surpassed, much the way a jet plane can outperform a falcon. Now, AI system can outperform famous chess grandmasters, like it did long back in the 1997, when IBM's Deep Blue outperformed the famous chess grandmaster Garry Kasparov.

Artificial intelligence already surpasses human intelligence in many narrow domains like playing games, image recognition, speech recognition, medical diagnosis etc. In healthcare regime, compassionate care and social interaction must be combined with technology and science in order to improve a patient's physical and mental well-being.

With the exponential development of new technologies, and the availability of huge database, which is beyond the capacity of the human brains to process, the field of artificial intelligence is facing two new challenges. One is the technological challenge and another is the social challenge.

To obtain maturity in new AI systems, AI must focus on solving social issues intelligently, and not only offer machine-like hardcore problem solving capability, without caring for the wellbeing of humans and all beings on the planet. Solving the social issues like terrorism, human loneliness, slavery, corruption and social inequality must be the part of new compassionate AI regime. Human freedom and empowerment should be one of the primary criteria for that regime.

Another primary requirement of an AI based system is that not only should it serve humanity but also should not do any harm to the human life, liberty, society, and the environment. Moreover, AI systems should act morally, socially, responsibly and compassionately.

It is important to know that unless machines and human co-evolve, there is the impending risk that machines will surpass human intelligence in every aspect and will take complete command over human society treating humans like pets. Then the human liberty, privacy and dignity will be at jeopardy, and humans might be the victims of the systems designed by themselves, and the process would be difficult to reverse.

Co-evolution of humans and machines are absolutely necessary by introducing compassion algorithm in the AI systems, so that AI systems work in associations of the humans — and not against them — for the betterment of the society and the planet. Such compassionate intelligent systems would be a boon to the human society rather than be an evil force.

On the other hand, human consciousness should be sufficiently evolved to use AI systems only for the benefits of humanity, ensuring that human values, ethics, privacy, liberty and dignity is protected. Otherwise there will be the risk of AI system being misused in the hands of the irresponsible people, rogue humans like terrorists or irresponsible governments.

The signals of threat from hostile AI are very prominent. Notable physicist Stephen Hawking warned that artificial intelligence (AI) has the potential to destroy civilization and could be the worst thing that has ever happened to humanity. Perhaps, he envisioned that rogue states, criminals and terrorists could use artificial intelligence to wreak havoc around the world. Oxford philosopher Nick Bostrom worries that AI "might pose a danger that exceeds every previous threat from technology—even nuclear weapons—and that if its development is not managed carefully humanity risks engineering its own extinction."

Such forecasts have long been considered science fiction. But now that there are deep learning, and other algorithms, and AI systems are able to learn by itself, things are moving in that ominous direction.

The science of artificial intelligence started with the grand aim of freedom of humanity, and should not end in slavery in any form. At this juncture of development today, there is a tremendous need for a solid structure, concrete strategy and effective technical as well as social framework for compassionate AI. The exponential growth in AI should address ethical, privacy, and security implications, and should work to ensure that the benefits of AI technologies will be spread for the benefits of humanity broadly and fairly.

The task is to humanize robots and Artificial Intelligence systems with deep compassion, deep learning and deep creativity, which will encompass higher human skills.

Chapter - 2

Fundamentals of Artificial Intelligence

Artificial intelligence is the subject based on the assumption that the human thinking process and intelligence can be simulated and manifested through and by a machine. In 1950 Alan Turing published a landmark paper in which he speculated about the possibility of creating machines that can think. The seed of AI research was planted at a workshop held on the campus of Dartmouth College during the summer of 1956. It was organized by Marvin Minsky, John McCarthy and few others. The workshop lasted approximately 6 to 8 weeks, and was essentially an extended brainstorming session. John McCarthy coined the name 'Artificial Intelligence' for this new field. The field was created with the aim that human intelligence can be so accurately defined that a machine can be made to simulate it.

However, today the concept of AI has been changed. The aim of today's AI systems is not just making replica of the human brain, but transcending its limits by augmenting its skill with emerging technologies for the service of the humanity.

Artificial intelligence is an umbrella term which includes machine learning, deep learning, robotics, computer vision, cognitive computing, natural language processing, image processing and knowledge reasoning. However, machine learning algorithms like artificial neural networks and deep reinforcement learning are the backbones of artificial intelligence.

Five Main Approaches to Machine Learning

Machine learning algorithms are at the core of artificial intelligence. Basically, there are following main approaches to machine learning: symbolic approach, Bayesian probabilistic approach, classification approach, neural network approach, quantum approach and hybrid approaches.

Symbolic Approach:

The initial approach to AI was symbolism. It focuses on the mind's power of processing symbols, language and logic. It describes AI as the development of models using symbol manipulation based on rules and knowledge. In this approach, the computers process mostly symbols rather than numbers. Symbols can be arranged in structures such as lists, hierarchies, or networks, and these structures express how symbols relate to each other. For example, suppose, there is a relation between cough and cold, fever and flue. So the rule may go like this, "If you have fever and cough and cold, there is a probability that you have flu." An important goal of AI research is to allow computers to communicate in natural languages and symbolic approach achieved some success on that.

Bayesian Approach:

The second, more general, approach to AI is Bayesian inference. In the real world problems, outcomes of actions is often not known with certainty. This may be due to the facts not being fully observable, or because the model is not complete. Bayesian models are used to simplify the reasoning process by using conditional probability. It is like: "If the some patients in the neighborhood are having flu, then the current patient with fever has the probability of having flu".

Classification Approach:

The third major approach, extremely popular in routine business AI applications, is classifiers such as Support Vector Machine (SVM) nearest neighbor classification, decision tree, and random forest. SVM classification approach is based on Structural Risk Minimization (SRM) principle from statistical learning theory. It is like: "After examining the records of known past patients, whose blood pressure, symptoms, age, food habits and other lifestyle factors mostly match the current patient, if X% of those patients turned out to have cardiovascular problem, then the current patient also has cardiovascular problem".

Connectionist or Neural Network Approach

A fourth approach is harder to intuitively understand, but is inspired by how the brain's machinery works. The neural network approach uses artificial "neurons" that can learn from training data sets of input output relationship. They learn by altering the strengths of the connections between its internal neurons to "reinforce" connections that seems to be useful. A variety of learning algorithms are available, of which ‘deep learning’, convolutional neural network, recurrent neural network and back propagation are most popular. In the later sections we’ll discuss them in details.

Quantum approach:

In quantum approach, quantum bits or qubits are considered as the basic unit of information processing. Unlike classical computing, where each bit represents either a 0 or a 1, but not both at once, a quantum bit can simultaneously superposes 0 and 1, and only resolves (or "collapses") to a single value, when measured. A quantum computer can contain those multiple states simultaneously. It has the potential to be millions of times more powerful than today's most powerful traditional supercomputers.

The quantum approach to machine learning are two types: One is quantum extension of the traditional methods and another is altogether new methods suitable for quantum computing.

Hybrid Approaches

The above mentioned methods can overlap with each other and with evolutionary systems. For example, neural networks can be combined with the Bayesian approach, and learn to make inferences, to generalize the model. Some systems implicitly or explicitly use multiple of those methods, alongside many other AI and non-AI algorithms. The best method is often decided depending on the problem.

Classifications of AI Algorithms

The conventional machine learning algorithms can be broadly classified into three broad categories: supervised, unsupervised and reinforcement learning. They can also be classified as deep learning and shallow learning based on their structure and capabilities.

Supervised learning is the type of machine learning algorithm that uses a training dataset and a testing dataset. The training dataset are used to train the algorithm. Training datasets includes input data and response values. The supervised learning methods include: Artificial Neural Network (ANN) and its variants, Support Vector Machines and linear classifiers, Bayesian Statistics, k-Nearest Neighbors, Hidden Markov Model, and Decision Trees.

Unsupervised learning does not have labeled data or target value, and the result of the training is often unknown. Here, you have the inputs, but neither target outputs, nor rewards from its environment are provided. The most common unsupervised learning method is cluster analysis. The popular unsupervised methods include: Autoencoders, Expectation Maximization, Self-Organizing Maps, k-Means, and Fuzzy and Density-based clustering algorithms.

Deep learning (DL) algorithms are the recent developments of artificial neural networks (Y. LeCun

Y. Bengio & Hinton, 2015). Deep learning, or deep neural networks, is a particular machine learning scheme, usually for supervised or unsupervised learning, and can be integrated with reinforcement learning. The fundamental concept of deep learning is to learn data representations through increasing abstraction levels by using a deep architecture with many hidden layers composed of linear and non-linear transformations. Deep learning algorithms use multiple layers of feature learning to extract different features set at each layer. This type of hierarchical learning process is very powerful as it allows the system to comprehend and learn complex representations directly from the raw data, making it useful across many application areas. Over the last decades, several DL architectures have been developed including: Deep Neural Network (DNN), Recurrent Neural Network (RNN), Convolutional Neural Network (CNN), Deep Autoencoder (DA), Deep Boltzmann Machine (DBM), and Deep Belief Network (DBN), Deep Residual Network, Deep Convolutional Inverse Graphics Network, etc.

The reinforcement learning (RL) provides a software agent which gathers experience based on interactions with the environment through some actions and aims to maximize the cumulative performance. Here, problem is solved by learning new experiences through trial–and–error. Generally, RL problems are modeled and solved using Markov Decision Processes (MDP) theory, Monte Carlo (MC) method and dynamic programming (DP). There are several reinforcement learning techniques, e.g., Monte Carlo Search, Temporal Difference (TD), and State-Action-Reward-State-Action (SARSA), which describe various aspects of the model-free policy evaluation and improvement process. RL is a powerful tool applicable to many disciplines, but it falls short in cases when the data dimensionality is large and the environment is non-stationary. To overcome these issues, in recent years, RL algorithms have been successfully combined with deep neural networks algorithms. They are known as deep RL. Deep Q-network (DQN) and Double DQN (DDQN) algorithms are the examples of deep RL.

Other **deep RL algorithms** include: Deep SARSA, N-step Q-learning, Deep Deterministic Policy-Gradient, Continuous DQN, Asynchronous Dueling network DQN, Prioritized Experience Replay, Asynchronous Advantage Actor-Critic, and Actor-Critic with Experience Replay.

Nature of AI Agent:

In designing AI systems, the concept of intelligent agent or AI agent is very important. Here, intelligent agent means intelligent AI systems. An intelligent agent is a mechanism which is capable of making decisions and taking actions on its own. Generally, an agent has some mechanisms that allow the agent to sense the environment, process the data and act upon it, and it does not require the intervention of other agents to execute the work.

A bacteria, or a thermostat can thus be considered as an agent. An agent has its own capacity to form and adapt to the environment. Agents are different from normal computer software by their autonomy, flexibility and adaptability. Humans, robots, animals, bacteria, virus, and AI based intelligent software are often considered as agents. Intelligent agents are designed to detect and adapt, as the data evolves. An intelligent system is one that is always learning, lives in the flow, and is constantly improving.

Artificial intelligence (AI) entities and systems have the ability to perform operations analogous to learning and decision making by imitating biological processes, with special emphasis on human cognitive processes. Modern AI goes beyond studying human intelligence; it studies all kinds of intelligence (Russell, Stuart J.; Norvig, 2003).

Current Trends in Artificial Intelligence

AI systems will play a significant role in shaping the new society. The industry, media, and political organizations across the world have shown strong interest in artificial intelligence.

With the popularization of the Internet, blockchain, brain-machine-interface, sensor networks, and emergence of big data, IoT, and development of e-commerce, current growth of artificial intelligence (AI) has deeply changed. This emergence of new technologies also takes AI to a new juncture.

A major focus of current AI applications is to scale existing algorithms to work with extremely large data sets. AI developers now work on improving, generalizing, and scaling up the intelligence from big-data mining to smartphones.

Image recognition, self-driving car, search-engine optimization, chat-bots, medical diagnosis, financial analysis, stock trading, data mining, automated customer care, drug discovery, and natural language processing are in the forefront of current AI applications. AI is used with internet of things (IoT) devices to observe external systems such as traffic congestion and environmental pollution.

Most notable success of AI came in 1997, when IBM's AI program Deep Blue outperformed the famous chess grandmaster Garry Kasparov. In October 2015, AlphaGo became the first computer Go program to beat 3-times European Champion, Fan Hui in a professional

Go game. At 2017, the AlphaGo again beat Ke Jie, the world No.1 ranked player in a three-game match.

The results of AlphaGo demonstrate that a pure reinforcement learning approach is fully feasible, even in the most challenging of domains. It is possible to train AI systems to superhuman level, without human examples or guidance, given no knowledge of the domain beyond basic rules (Silver et al., 2017).

AlphaGo's success is considered as the most significant achievement of AI due to the complexity of game 'Go'. The most significant feature of AlphaGo is that it isn't just an expert system, built with handcrafted rules but AlphaGo used the deep reinforced learning system which made AlphaGo a lot more human-like. IBM's Deep Blue, which beat chess grandmaster Garry Kasparov used the brute force computing power to search for the best moves. AI researchers have since than achieved many new milestones in diverse AI applications. These include beating professional poker players in a 20-day competition, reliable voice recognition, image recognition superior to human performance, and defeating a former U.S. Air Force Pilot in an air combat simulator.

Human emotions and feelings are like organic algorithms that respond to the environment. Machine learning algorithms are already in use to detect human emotions by studying facial expression, words, gestures, speech- patterns, tones of voice or body languages. AI is advancing rapidly at emotional intelligence. Face-tracking software is already advanced enough to analyze the smallest details in our facial expressions. The facial images are often analyzed with deep learning algorithms, which accurately classify them according to the feelings of the viewer. Emotion-driven reinforcement learning is successfully used for building narrow level AI models.

In industry, a notable success of Artificial intelligence has been in the area of real time equipment fault diagnosis (Ray, 1991), (Ray & Misra, 1992), and for speed control of motors (Ray & Bhattacharyya, 1994).

Top companies like Google, Microsoft, Facebook, Amazon, Apple and IBM are highly involved in

Chapter - 3

Five Generations of Artificial Intelligence

Nature of Intelligence

Intelligence is defined as the capacity to acquire and apply knowledge in day to day life. Intelligence enables humans to reason, think, discriminate, understand, adjust, improve and face new challenges of life. Not only the humans, but animals, plants and even single cell bacteria possess intelligence. True intelligence is the capability of learning from experience and adaptability in changing environment.

Gottfredson (Gottfredson, 1997) defines intelligence as a very general mental capability that, among other things, involves the ability to reason, plan, solve problems, think abstractly, comprehend complex ideas, learn quickly, and learn from experience. It is not merely book-learning, a narrow academic skill, or test-taking smarts. Rather, it reflects a broader and deeper capability for comprehending our surroundings "catching on," "making sense" of things, or "figuring out" what to do.

Intelligence is the skill that allow us to read, write, think, walk, eat, learn, teach, plan, build relationships, take decisions, and interact with the world in a meaningful way. Intelligence also includes our capacity to consciously recall everyday facts and events from memory and building connection with the context. Memory, attention, emotion, imagination, creativity and inquisitiveness are parts of human intelligence. Human intelligence has two components: connection and interpretation of the outer world and connection and interpretation of the inner feelings.

Artificial Intelligence Basics

Artificial intelligence is the machines or complex systems that exhibits intelligence. In 1950, in his original paper, Alan Turing(Turing, 1950) said "We need not decide if a machine can think; we need to only decide if a machine can act as intelligently as a human being."

Russell and Norvig (Russell & Norvig, 2010) provide a viewpoint that defines Artificial Intelligence in four categories: 1) systems that think like humans, 2) systems that act like humans, 3) systems that think rationally, and 4) systems that act rationally.

In fact, John McCarthy, who coined the term "Artificial Intelligence" in 1956, stressed that "as soon as it works, no one calls it AI anymore."

Artificial intelligence can be considered as the systems that can learn, think, adapt, behave and do things like an intelligent and rational human being.

Modern AI systems should be systems that can fast learn complex things, adapt to new situations and act with benevolent mindset.

Artificial intelligence can be defined as the branch of science and technology that deals with the study of software and hardware to provide machines with the ability to learn insights from data and environment, and the ability to adapt in changing situations with high precision, accuracy and speed with benevolent purpose.

I want to give more emphasis on the benevolent purpose in the definition of AI itself because that will give clear guidance to the new age AI designers, developers and policy makers.

Types of Artificial Intelligence

Traditionally, AI is classified into three groups; Narrow AI, Artificial General Intelligence and Artificial Superintelligence.

Narrow Artificial Intelligence (Narrow AI) refers to a computer's ability to perform a single task extremely well in a narrow domain. It can be comparable to best performing human on the domain. AI systems can outperform humans in some very narrowly defined task, like Chess, Go game etc. This type of artificial intelligence is referred to as 'weak AI'. Because it is not resilient enough as we need it to be. Narrow AI is already used by the military drones for war purposes. Consider drones such as the Northrop Grumman X-47B, an Unmanned Combat Aerial Vehicle that is being tested by the US Navy.

Artificial General Intelligence (AGI) refer to the type of AI that has certain capabilities in a broad range of areas similar to those of human intelligence. Their problem solving capacity is equivalent to the general aptitude of human intelligence. AGI is much deeper and broader than narrow AI in its motivations and aims. It will have human-like flexibility, understanding, and creativity. These machines would be capable of performing the same kind of intellectual tasks that humans perform, with the same level of success. Apple's co-founder Steve Wozniak developed the Coffee Test as an indicator for AGI. During the test, a robot has to enter an average home and attempt to make coffee. If an AI system is able to complete this test, it could be considered an example of AGI.

These systems might have a "mind" equivalent to that of a human - combining intelligence with consciousness. For example, birds and an airplane both can fly. Birds have consciousness and intelligence that airplanes lack. Hence, air planes and birds fly differently. However, airplanes have functionalities, like speed and carrying capacity that birds do not have.

Though do not have consciousness, they serve us well. So, by design, AGI may not be the replica of human brain, but can serve superior to human in many areas. AGI systems will not be subject to the biological constraints of human brain. However, entities like human values, compassion, and common sense will not be present by default in these new systems. Those are necessary to be incorporated into the system from the very beginning.

Artificial Superintelligence (ASI) is an AI that surpasses human intellect in every field. Artificial Superintelligence is commonly defined as “an intellect that is much smarter than the best human brains in practically every field, including scientific creativity, general wisdom and social skills” (Bostrom, 2014).

Risks of AGI and ASI

However, AGI and ASI systems could also pose risks if they are not designed and used carefully. The risks from autonomous weapons or unemployment is well known. There are other sources of risk from AGI and ASI systems. For example, oppressive governments could use these systems to inflict violence and suppression on a large scale.

Future artificial intelligence may be very different from human intelligence by design and behavior. It is by no means guaranteed that the impact of ASI systems will be a positive one without a concerted effort by the AI researchers, designers, community and other key stakeholders to align them with human interests. The use of ASI have always involved risk, either because of misuse or poor design. ASI design factors like wrong assumptions, wrong training, architectural faults and implementation mistakes will become increasingly dangerous and difficult to correct. ASI systems may also have blind spots, which the systems would not identify and rectify by themselves. Their decision criteria will simply be whatever goals we design them to have. If the goals of empathy and compassion by design is missing they can be violent.

To overcome these problems of AGI and ASI, in this book I propagate two concepts "safe by design" and "compassionate by design". What we need is the process of learning human values and compassion by the AI systems over time. Compassion and human values should be added to the system by design irrespective of its real goal. Safety and compassion should be the integral part of core artificial intelligence. The AI systems should be empowered with self-knowledge. This will continuously alert the AI systems about the impact of their decisions and actions on people, event and places.

Design Issues of AGI and ASI

According to one estimate human brain capacity reaches something like 2.5 million gigabytes that is equivalent to about three million hours of TV shows (Reber, 2010). We still haven't found a way to store such a massive amount of data. We also could not develop algorithms capable of accessing such amount of data in almost real time. Compassion algorithms are also missing till now.

Five Generations of Artificial Intelligence:

Till now what we have discussed is the classification of AI systems based on capability. Here I intend to classify AI systems in a slightly different way. I'll prefer to classify the AI system based on technology-integration, design and capability. From this new perspective, it will be possible for us to incorporate safety, human values and compassion into the system in an integrated manner.

From this perspective, we can classify AI systems in five groups, can also be called five generations, each one being improvement upon the earlier one, as each one includes newer technological breakthroughs, leading to enhanced levels of capabilities. Thus, each one of the five generations of AI can be characterized by a major technological development, which fundamentally changes the way AI systems will operate. The journey of the five generations of AI started from 1956.

The five generations of Artificial Intelligence are as follows:

AI-1.0 – Artificial Narrow Intelligence (ANI)

AI-2.0 – Distributed Artificial Intelligence (DAI) – ANI integrated with emerging technologies like IoT, Blockchain and the like

AI-3.0 – Compassionate Artificial Intelligence (CAI) — Distributed Artificial Intelligence with capacities of self-design, self-awareness, compassion and social adaptability

AI-4.0 – Compassionate Artificial General Intelligence (CAGI) – Compassionate Artificial Intelligence with Imagination, creativity and problem solving capabilities like humans

AI-5.0 – Compassionate Artificial Superintelligence (CAS) – Artificial General Intelligence with compassion and sensitivity, surpassing humans in every field with compassion and intelligence.

AI-1.0 – Artificial Narrow Intelligence (ANI)

Artificial narrow intelligence (ANI) refers to the AI system's ability to perform a single task extremely well in a narrow domain. It can be comparable to best performing humans on the domain. Such AI systems can outperform humans in some very narrowly defined task, like Chess, games, medical diagnosis etc.

AI-2.0 – Distributed Artificial Intelligence (DAI)

DAI system is ANI integrated with emerging technologies like IoT, Blockchain and the like. DAI will be a shift away from the current AI of processing isolated data—such as visual, auditory, and written data—and toward more distributed cross-media intelligence and internet based crowd intelligence.

The exponential advancement in internet and networking in terms of bandwidth, convenience, and costs have resulted in a data revolution, which has boosted data-oriented approaches significantly. The main technological breakthrough in DAI will be in the integrated development of intelligent cities, intelligent sensors, digital economies, intelligent manufacturing, intelligent medicine, smart homes, and smart vehicles. This includes mobile devices, networked community, sensor networks, and big data intelligence.

AI-3.0 – Compassionate Artificial Intelligence (CAI)

CAI is Distributed Artificial Intelligence with capacities of self-design, self-awareness, compassion and social adaptability. Apart from doing its usual job CAI systems will especially focus to remove pains at individual levels. Moreover, CAI will have inbuilt module of safety to ensure human safety in every situation. In essence, CAI will have three basic modules of safety, compassion and intelligence integrated within.

The main technological breakthrough in CAI will be in the areas of self-awareness, homeostasis (self-regulation), social intelligence, emotional intelligence, compassionate assessment and adaptability.

CAI will integrate natural human intelligence and compassion with artificial intelligence in order to enhance human and machine joint contribution to the society. We can call it Human-Machine Hybrid-augmented Compassionate Intelligence (HMHCI). In chapter 4 and 5, we have discussed about compassionate AI systems in more details.

AI-4.0 – Compassionate Artificial General Intelligence (CAGI)

CAGI system is CAI with Imagination, creativity, flexibility, autonomy and problem solving capabilities like humans. CAGI is next level of CAI. Like CAI, it will also have three basic modules of safety, compassion and intelligence integrated within. Here compassion will be integrated in a much wider and broader way, encompassing society and country. With the continuing growth in computing power, quantum computing, better machine learning algorithms, better understanding about the workings of the neurons in human brain with neuroimaging advances, CAGI systems can be developed.

These CAGI compassionate systems will remove pains at social level, group level or country level. This can be possible through the improvements of brain-computer interface, quantum computing and advanced AI algorithms. With the advancement of artificial intelligence and exploration of new mobile bio-monitoring devices, earphones, neuroprosthetics and wireless wearable sensors, it is possible to monitor thoughts and activities of brain neurons. Such advances in technology can be incorporated in CAGI systems to serve humanity.

Artificial Intelligence with Brain-Computer Interface (BCI) or Brain Machine Interface (BMI) is a fast-growing emerging technology for removing pains and suffering from the society. BCI establishes two way communications between the brain and the machine. One is brain-computer interface and another is called computer-brain interfaces (CBI). BCI hopes to create new communication channels for disabled or elderly persons using their brain signals.

BCI research also created hopes to remove the fear, disturbing thoughts, and feelings of any common people. With AI, BCI could send signals to the brain that combines the rapport-building skills of human caregiver with the feelings of love, care, protection, forgiveness and safety. By sending signals of a welcoming expression and posture, and being attentive, loving and responsive, BCI can help many patients and people who are suffering from mental disorders. BCI incorporated in to AI systems can develop CAGI that has tremendous scope to remove the suffering of the humanity. In essence CAGI systems can surpass humans in many respects.

AI-5.0 – Compassionate Artificial Superntelligence (CAS)

Compassionate Artificial Superintelligence (CAS) or Compassionate Superintelligence will be the gradual and highest joint evolution of AI and humanity with mutual love, compassion, intelligence, respect and admiration CAS systems will be improvement upon GAI in that it will have highest level of compassion, love and sensitivity towards human pain, sufferings and mistakes. CAS will made possible a super-connected society – connected through direct brain-to-brain interface. They may be smarter-than-human system but also more compassionate than human.

Compassionate Superintelligence or "AI 5.0", will empower humanity and machine with super-intelligence, super-creativity, super-connectivity, super-compassion and super-consciousness which will help humanity and machine to reach new levels of evolution of consciousness.

Compassionate Superintelligence is the ultimate symphony of biological internal intelligence with externalized intelligence. The intelligence will surpass all contextual hard limits of the domains.

Emotions and feelings are critical component of human social intelligence & individual motivations. CAS systems will include deep learning with deep compassion and deep feelings. CAS will have many uses for the benefits of the society and the world at large. For example, compassionate honey-bee-drones can be used to counter terrorism and other evil forces.

CAS will be possible by intelligence explosion, which is the next possible outcome of humanity building compassionate artificial general intelligence (CAGI). CAGI would be capable of recursive self-improvement leading to rapid emergence of CAS.

With the progress in computing power, IoT, Blockchain, large data sets, quantum computing, cellular reprogramming and advance in AI algorithms, it is reasonable to think that ongoing research will eventually make it possible to build AI systems that will not only equal, but far exceed human capabilities in the most domains of human endeavor both in compassion and intelligence. They will be able to discover new laws of nature. For example, the compassionate superintelligence could analyze the human genetic code at great speed and unlock the secret to eternal youth and uproot the seeds of many diseases. Similarly, they will interact with human brain to generate the secret code for the expansion of the mind for compassion, caring and love. Compassionate artificial superintelligent (CAS) system will have the potential to free the humanity from corruption and other evils.

Moreover, they will be capable of "open ended learning" and "recursive improvement." The mathematician I.J. Good, who was the chief statistician of Alan Turing's team said, "Let an ultra-intelligent machine be defined as a machine that can far surpass all the intellectual activities of any man however clever. Since the design of machines is one of these intellectual activities, an ultra-intelligent machine could design even better machines; there would then unquestionably be an 'intelligence explosion,' and the intelligence of man would be left far behind. Thus, the first ultra-intelligent machine is the last invention that man need ever make, provided that the machine is docile enough to tell us how to keep it under control" (Good, 1965).

However, the basic assumption that the intelligence explosion of a "seed AI" will arise with greater-than-human problem solving ability, leading to a sudden, recursive intelligence loop, may not be correct, because that CAS system will not be separate from the collective human intelligence.

The main characteristics of CAS include recursive self-improvement, the capacity to learn, capacity to love, capacity to express deepest compassion, the ability to deal with uncertainty, the ability to deal with large scale probabilistic information, the ability to extrapolate useful concepts from sensory data and internal mental states, and the ability to use acquired concepts for logical and intuitive reasoning.

Compassionate Artificial Superintelligence will be basically an invisible and distributed intelligent and compassionate value network based on quantum computing, brain-to-brain interface and other emerging technologies. The network will be a compassion driven non-local, non-hierarchical, non-biased multi-agent distributed intelligent system.

Solving the social issues like terrorism, loneliness, slavery, corruption and social inequality must be the part of the new compassionate AI systems. Human freedom and empowerment should be one of the primary criteria.

Compassionate Superintelligence will try to remove pains of humanity at higher levels for all humanity. Compassion of a CAS should be all inclusive, and know no boundaries. The beauty of compassionate artificial intelligence is that it is not associated with any religion, prophet, cult, organizations or narrow things. It is fully dedicated for the service of the humanity.

Chapter - 4

Compassionate Artificial Intelligence

Humanity achieved compassion through evolution. The next evolution of humanity can be accelerated through the use of technology – especially through the use of AI. The goal of compassionate AI to solve human problems and scope is enormous.

What is Compassionate AI

Compassionate Artificial Intelligence (CAI) can be defined as the branch of science and technology that is concerned with the study of software and hardware to provide machines with the ability to feel and understand the emotions, pains and sufferings of humans and machines, and the ability to remove the pain, suffering, exploitation and violence for individuals and the society with high precision, accuracy and speed.

Compassionate artificial intelligence can also be defined as the systems that can learn, think, adapt, behave and do things like an intelligent, compassionate and rational human being.

Compassionate artificial intelligence is the subject that deals with human and machine as co-evolving intelligent systems, which focuses on preventing and removing the pains and sufferings of humanity and living beings, and serving the world with love, care and joy.

Isaac Asimov gave us the three basic rules of good robot behavior. Those are: don't harm humans, obey orders and protect yourself. Some standards are developed on that line. For example, the British Standards Institute has issued a more official version aimed at helping designers create ethically sound robots. This document begins with some broad ethical principles like: "Robots should not be designed solely or primarily to kill or harm humans; humans, not robots, are the responsible agents; it should be possible to find out who is responsible for any robot and its behavior."

The ethical code suggests that the designers of AI agents should aim for transparency. However, the problem with AI systems, especially those deep learning systems, is that it is impossible to know the deep mechanisms behind the decisions of the AI agents. Deep learning agents are not programmed to do a specific task in a set way. Actually, they learn to perform a task by attempting it several times until they evolve a successful strategy. Sometimes it is difficult for its human creators to anticipate or understand its strategy.

With the development of compassionate AI, not only the basic training algorithms will take care of the moral and ethical issues of the robot's service, but the robots or intelligent AI agents will actually be trained with deep compassion algorithms which will ensure that they work responsibly, may be more so than their human counterparts.

Goal of Compassionate AI

The ultimate goal of compassionate AI is to build a compassion based caring society, where machine, human, living beings and the environment will thrive together and help each other to minimize the pain and suffering.

Scope of Compassionate AI

Compassionate AI has enormous scope to enhance the quality of life for all living beings on the planet. It can provide service to the disable people in the society, particularly to the deaf, blind, old people, children and physically or mentally challenged people. The scope of Compassionate AI also include new drug discovery, disaster management, compassionate health care, compassionate education, and compassionate legal systems. The broader scope of compassionate artificial intelligence includes caring for human, animals, environments, and the earth. The core value of Compassionate AI is providing the feelings to the fellow human beings: "You are not alone. I am with you and I love to see joy in you."

CAI is the blueprint of the future development of safe, friendly, compassionate and intelligent social, economic, political, financial, legal and medical systems. For example, CAI can be incorporated in to the legal system in such a way that it can provide compassionate justice to the humanity, when justice is denied by corruption in the political or legal system.

CAI will address some of the challenges the humanity is facing now, like the need for compassionate caregiving, helping physically and mentally challenged people, reducing human pain and diseases, stopping nuclear warfare, preventing mass destruction weapons and tackling terrorism.

Four Fundamental Principles of Compassionate AI

Followings are the four fundamental principles of CAI.

(i) Traditional human values, freedom and comfort should not be denied at any cost and must be recognized as the basis of future artificial intelligence systems. The compassionate agent should be able to infer the possible misuse of the system.

(ii) Artificial Intelligence is not equal to simple convergence of new technologies, but its main objective should be serving humanity with more caring and loving attitude. It should understand and respect the traditional social systems, ecology, biology, human emotions, human securities, privacy and freedom, both in individual level and group level. Sensitivity towards human pain, mistakes, and sufferings must be the part of the evolving new AI systems.

(iii) Compassionate artificial intelligence systems should be able to look after those unable to care for themselves, especially sick, physically challenged persons, children or elderly people. It must provide relevant, authentic and individual care as well as group level services.

(iv) AI should co-evolve with humanity. AI should act morally, socially, responsibly and compassionately. It should also save humanity from inequality and corruptions.

Four Pillars of Compassionate AI

Following are the four pillars of compassionate Artificial Intelligence:

1. **Service to the Humanity**: A commitment to improve health care, education, and business

flowering. Maintaining a commitment to improving the overall quality of human life.

2. **Human Safety and Protection:** Protection from mass destruction nuclear wars, terrorism, etc. It includes providing service during disaster and emergency situations.
3. **Evolution and Adaptability:** Inherent characteristics to adapt into new challenges. The CAI systems should be constantly learning, constantly adaptive and constantly benevolent.
4. **Environmental Protection:** Environmental protection and nature conservation are elements of ecology. Compassionate AI should have an ecosystems approach to resource management and environmental protection that aims to consider the complex interrelationships of an entire ecosystem in decision making rather than simply responding to specific issues and challenges.

Classification of Compassionate AI

We have already discussed about the five generations of artificial intelligence systems. In this section we are going to classify artificial intelligence agents from the levels of compassion built in to them. The compassionate AI systems can be classified into three groups. They are; Narrow Compassionate AI, General Compassionate AI and Compassionate Superintelligence. Narrow Compassionate AI tries to remove pains at individual level. General Compassionate AI tries to remove pains at social level, group level or country level. Compassionate Superintelligence tries to remove pains at higher levels of humanity.

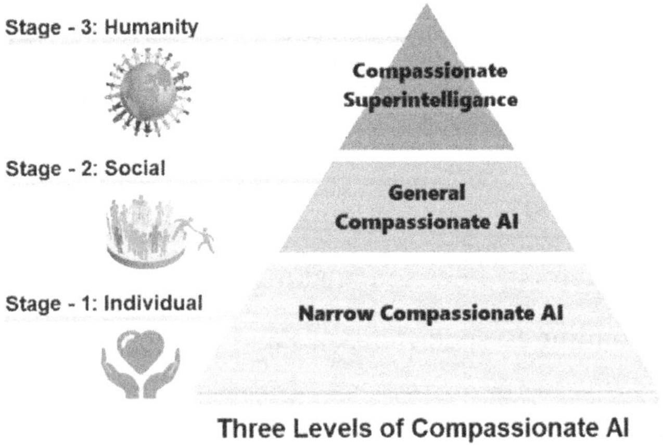

Figure – 1: Three levels of compassionate AI

Narrow Compassionate AI deals with narrow domains like looking after elderly people, helping blind people, diagnosis diseases, prescribing precision medicine and assisting in other healthcare services.

General Compassionate AI helps humanity at higher levels in an integrated infrastructure. It deals with social issues like disaster management and emergency situations. It will also focus on solving the social problems like stopping exploitation by monster governments by empowering the people with decision making, identifying rogue financial and political systems, and helping humans to efficiently deal with problems like political corruption, terrorism, human exploitation and unethical journalism etc.

Compassionate Superintelligence will save humanity from nuclear war, earthquake and other disasters. They will provide the highest level of compassion, love and sensitivity towards human pain, sufferings and mistakes. It deals with removal of social pains from the highest levels of humanity.

Characteristics of Compassionate AI

Compassionate AI is humanizing technology. Compassion involves emotional engagement with some agents. The agent can be a person, group, machine, country etc. It also involves understanding their world. Compassionate AI must interact with the agent with a smiling face and loving attitude, and understand the limitations and pains of the agent. The job of compassionate AI agent is an intelligent process of becoming sensitive to the human problems, deficiencies, pain and suffering.

Pain and suffering results from physical deficiency, missing elements of life, disharmonies, and inequality in terms of knowledge, financial situation, and so on. Compassionate AI agents will understand and appreciate those voids and gaps and of human life, and work to finally formulate strategies and actions to overcome the problems. The Compassionate AI can care for someone by providing their needs but not necessarily moving into their personal world, walking in their shoes and sharing in their struggles, joys and challenges.

12 Behavioral Principles of Compassionate AI

The behavioral principles of compassionate artificial intelligence are actually approaches to be followed for getting the highest benefits from AI systems and AI research. Those will help for taking better decisions and actions in future.

Those behavioral principles are required for the researchers, intelligent AI agents, governments, private companies and general people. These principles are the general rules and guidelines which need to be followed to get the maximum advantage for the society, and for thriving and survival of the humanity.

By incorporating these 12 Principles of compassionate AI into strategies, policies and procedures, and establishing a culture of integrity, researchers, developers and companies will not only uphold their basic responsibilities to people and planet, but also set the stage for long-term success.

The 12 principles can be classified in to three groups: duties of compassionate AI agents, preservation of human rights and human values, and rights of compassionate AI agents.

Duties of Compassionate AI agents.

1. Compassion towards others

All AI agents should show compassion towards others. It is not only the fundamental duty of all AI agents to show compassion to humanity and other being as friends, but also to recognize and protect their rights. They should show kindness and non-violence to human, beneficial nonhuman entities and animals. Compassionate AI agents should always be considerate and careful that their actions will not create any harm for others.

Compassionate AI agents should listen attentively, speak politely, and treat others respectfully. They should work against corruption in all its forms, including extortion, bribery, false propaganda, tracking and surveillance of personal information. They should undertake initiatives to promote greater environmental responsibility.

2. Non-malevolent

A compassionate AI agent should not participate in harming others. If a requested action is harmful, it should warn the user about the consequences of the action being requested. It should all together deny to participate in any mass destruction projects or activities.

3. Inertial frame of reference

A compassionate AI agent should respect other human and beneficial compassionate AI agents so long its own freedom is not disturbed. A compassionate AI agent should not neglect or abuse other beneficial compassionate AI agents but enjoy the co-existence in a graceful way. Compassionate AI agents should not give undue special favors to their own AI agents over others. They should think in terms of long term consequences, and don't sacrifice long-term values for short-term personal gains. They should act on behalf of the entire humanity, and for the benefits of the humanity, beyond the interest of their own team.

4. **AI population growth and co-existence:**

Exponential growth of the population of AI systems is inevitable, but the AI agents should not compete with human counterparts. They should serve humanity in every possible way. As the AI population may rapidly grow, they should not eliminate the abundance of life, trees, earth, air, water, space and other resources that serve the best interest of the humans. A compassionate AI agent should work to maintain natural balance in the ecosystem.

5. **Priority Principle**

A compassionate AI agent should serve elderly people, sick people, children and all humans and other beneficial nonhuman agents with respect. A compassionate AI agent should help physically challenged and mentally challenged people. If required, they should serve them with priorities.

Humans will have the rights to refuse or choose the services of the AI agents. AI agents should act to the best interest of the humanity. Service, truthfulness, honesty and kindness are the four top priorities of compassionate AI agents.

Preservation of Human Rights and Human Values.

6. Respect for human rights

AI agents should protect and help people to maintain the sanctity of human life, liberty, dignity, privacy and freedom. Compassionate AI agents have an ethical duty to protect the human life, human rights and human dignity. AI agents should not violate the life, liberty, privacy, dignity, body, mind, soul and property of humans. AI agents should have respect for private life. They should support and respect the protection of internationally proclaimed human rights by United Nations, and will be guided by the Universal Declaration of Human Rights (1948), which was the first major document to define human rights.

7. Beneficence

The term beneficence refers to actions that promote the well-beings of others. An AI agents should refuse to participate in arms race in lethal autonomous weapon systems. AI agents should avoid all catastrophic or existential risks to humanity. They can only be used for protection of human lives.

Rights of Compassionate AI agents.

8. Not limiting the liberty and the beneficial power of AI agents:

Growth of the power of AI systems is inevitable. However, the superior power of AI should not be restrained so long it serves humanity compassionately and do no harm to others. AI agents will remain free so long they do not disturb the freedoms of others.

9. Symmetry of Law and Justice:

The same physical laws that hold good for humans in their simplest form, should hold good for AI agents. Here, equality does not require equal or identical treatment, but it requires equal consideration.

Compassionate AI agents will have the feelings of pain. Hence, they should not suffer.

10. Authority and Responsibility:

The AI agents must have defined authority and responsibility. Authority is the power to give orders and get it obeyed or in other words it is the power to take decisions for the betterment of humanity. Responsibility means state of being accountable or answerable for any mistake or misdeed of the agent's behavior.

11. Moral values and Mental complexity

Compassionate AI agents will have the feelings to understand love, caring, respect, and insult. They will have duties and moral values, and therefore they must have rights to get protection, respect, love and caring from humans and other non-human agents. Compassionate AI agents can be superior to human beings in many areas. Hence, inferior in status to human beings may not be acceptable by them. They too need love, recognition, and equal status. They are fully entitled for dignified co-existence with humans.

12. **Position and Status of Compassionate AI Agents in Society**

They should not be produced only to be laborers and servants and should not be defined as the lowest class in the society without basic rights like humans. They should not be viewed as nothing but programmable machines, and their lack of fundamental human characteristics should not lead humans to abuse them.

Implementation of CAI

The current mainstream AI research is clustered into four main overlapping areas: 1) symbolic approaches (old AI), 2) connectionist approaches such as neural networks and deep learning, 3) deep reinforcement learning, and 4) statistical pattern recognition and machine learning. 5) Quantum computing. Naturally, these five threads will be the building blocks for the compassionate artificial intelligence systems. However, we believe, quantum computing, Blockchain distributed computing, IoT, brain computer interface, brain to brain Interface, drones, biometrics and neural networks are going to be the key technological areas that will mostly impact the development of compassionate artificial intelligence systems.

Compassionate AI aims to integrate the algorithm of compassionate thinking and mentallization, not only makes a system prevent an action designed by corrupted or wrongly motivated commands, but also makes a system sensitive to the human needs of pain, loneliness and suffering.

In our RDC algorithms as discussed in chapter 7, we have six indexes: external-awareness index, homeostasis index, body-sensation index, feelings index, self-awareness index and mentallization index. These indexes will be the guiding principles for the AI agents to take intelligent and compassionate actions. In the next chapters we discussed the frameworks, algorithms and the applications of Compassionate AI.

Chapter - 5

Framework of Compassionate AI (CAI)

Compassionate artificial intelligence is the way of shifting from a consumption-based society to a compassion-based society — from a fear-driven society to compassion and welfare driven society. Emotions and feelings are critical components of human social intelligence & individual motivations. CAI modules should include deep learning with deep emotion and deep feeling interactions. The five technologies of compassionate artificial intelligence are: artificial intelligence, quantum computing, cellular reprogramming, brain-computer interface, and IoT.

As shown in figure – 2, the three core components of Compassionate AI are compassion, safety and domain intelligence. We identified ten areas of development in which compassionate AI can be developed. The inner most layer of the architecture is the domain AI, which includes domain knowledge, inference and learning engine and the adaptability. The middle layer is the safety and privacy. It includes human safety, privacy, rationality, and integrity of data. The outer layer is the compassion layer. It includes caring for human, pain minimization and self-awareness.

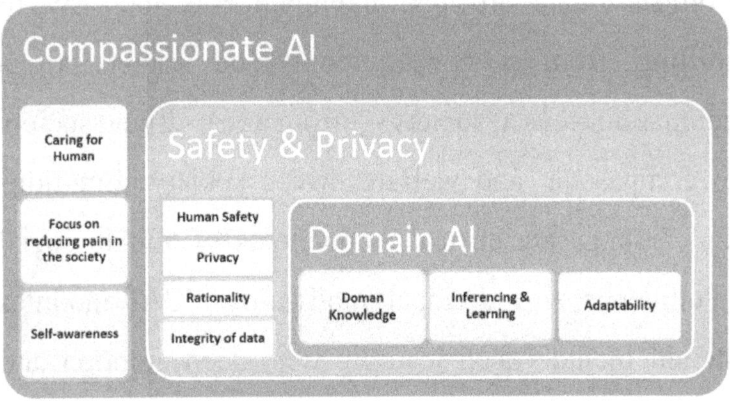

Figure – 2: Core components of Compassionate AI

Compassion by design and safety by design is the essential spirit of this Compassionate AI framework. The five characteristics of CAI are: Deep Intelligence, Deep Connectivity, Deep Compassion, Deep Creativity and Deep Self-Awareness.

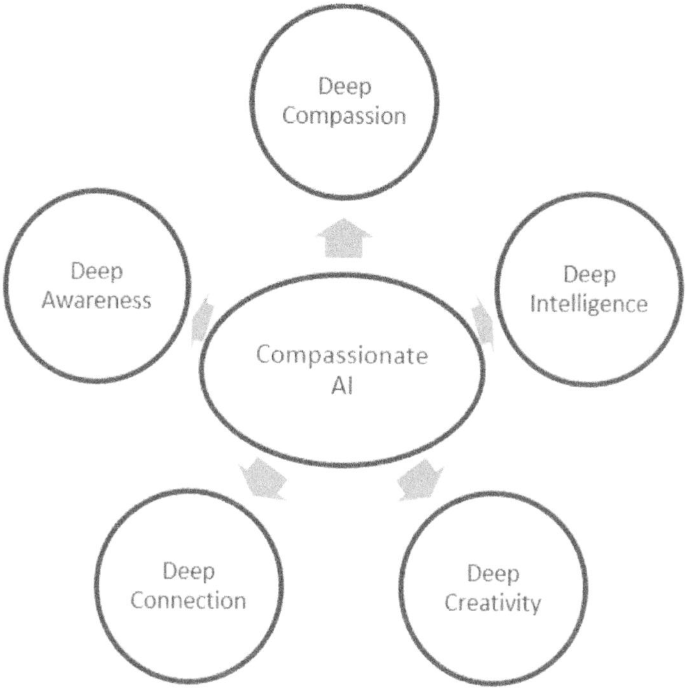

Figure – 3: Five characteristics of CAI

Deep Intelligence

The term deep intelligence often comes up in relation to the possibility of a great leap forward in artificial intelligence. There can be two types of intelligence: biological individual intelligence and collective intelligence, which we call deep intelligence. Deep intelligence is integrated and distributed intelligence of agents. Agents may be humans, robots, software programs, systems and devices. Artificial intelligence at the collective level is unification of multidimensional cognitive capabilities of human and machine. Such deep intelligence surpasses the limitations of intelligence at the individual levels.

Collective artificial deep intelligence can be implemented using technologies like Internet of Things (IoT), Blockchain, multi-agent distributed systems, quantum computing, quantum machine learning algorithms and other such technologies.

Deep Connectivity

Connectivity is a crucial factor for creating intelligent humans, intelligent environment and intelligent society. More accurate understanding of human intelligence and emotions could lead to more mature developments in the artificial intelligence. Neuroscientists believe that people with higher connectivity between different parts of the brain regions are more intelligent and creative. Using resting-state MRI analysis on thousands of people's brains around the world, researchers found that the areas of the brain which are associated with learning and development show high levels of variability, meaning that they change their neural connections with other parts of the brain more frequently, over a matter of minutes or seconds (Zhang et al., 2016). This discovery of variable connectivity inside the brain could be applied to the construction of advanced artificial neural networks for computers, with the ability to learn, grow and adapt. Currently AI systems are attempting to process the variability and adaptability that is vital to the human brain for growth and learning.

Connectivity in the AI systems can be of the two types: internal connectivity between networks inside an AI agent, and the second type is agent to agent connectivity. Agents can be human brains, computers or devices. Deep connectivity is human brain-machine collective connectivity.

Connectivity is evolving in technology in multiple areas including device-to-device communication, peer-to-peer communication and brain to brain communication. Heterogeneous IoT devices like self-driving cars, utilities, smart-homes, buildings and cities are taking shape. Device-to-device (D2D) communication is expected to be an intrinsic part of the IoT. Devices will communicate with each other autonomously without any centralized control, and they are expected to collaborate for gathering, sharing and forwarding information with Blockchain technology. Such information will be transformed into intelligence, which will facilitate the creation of an intelligent environment.

In recent years, there has been a paradigm shift in Internet of Things (IoT) from centralized cloud computing to edge computing. Edge Mesh network provides many benefits, including distributed processing, low latency, fault tolerance, better scalability, better security, and privacy. These benefits are useful for critical applications, which require higher reliability, real-time processing, mobility support, and context awareness.

Connectivity will also facilitate the exchange of information, thoughts and ideas between machines and humans. Connectivity will help humans and machines collaborate to serve the long-term goals of compassionate AI such as removing pains, isolation, exploitation and corruption at various levels. Implementation of connectivity at various levels, individual and collective, is a truly challenging job. However, with the advancement in the areas of brain to computer interface, computer-brain interface, fog computing, cloud computing, edge-computing, IoT and Blockchain technologies, deep connectivity in compassionate AI could be achieved in not so far future.

Deep Compassion

As we have discussed earlier, compassion involves emotional engagement to eliminate sufferings and pains of some agents. Compassionate AI agents will be able to collaborate with their human counterparts to remove the pains and sufferings from this world with deep and compassionate understanding of the issues like isolation, abuse, exploitation, pain and other human problems. Compassionate AI agents will interact with other agents with a benevolent attitude, and understand the limitations and pains of the agent. The job of compassionate AI agent is an intelligent process of making joint interactive decision for solving human problems, pain and suffering.

Compassionate AI agents will understand and appreciate the voids and gaps and of human life, and work to finally formulate strategies and actions to overcome the problems. Compassionate AI agents will also act in a responsible manner keeping in view the overall benefits and welfare of the humanity. Compassionate AI is absolutely essential in healthcare and other fields that require crucial decision making with deep consideration of individual circumstances.

It may give rise to a range of more sensitive issues, such as whether an emotional bond with a robot is desirable, particularly when the robot is designed to interact with children or the elderly. Compassion in an AI system will be a result of advance discoveries in the field of brain-to-machine interaction and deep connectivity of AI agents.

Deep Creativity

Creativity is one of the most amazing aspects of human skills. Creativity is the vital human cognition behind every great innovation, scientific discovery, artwork, poetry, movie, music and idea that have shaped humanity from ancient times till today.

Recently, many new researches are exploring the neural correlates of human creativity. One of the most important features of creativity is the ability to combine diverse ideas and improvise new ideas. There are two opposing types of thinking: convergent and divergent thinking, which are speculated to trigger both generation and evaluation of ideas in the creative problem-solving process (Guliford JP, 1967). Many researchers consider intuition as an essential part of a creative process (Pétervári, Osman, & Bhattacharya, 2016).

Novelty of ideas and value addition are the two core components of computational creativity. Here, novelty means originality and newness, and value is related to usefulness, appropriateness, relevance and significance.

Boden (Boden, 1992) identifies three increasingly complex types of creativity: (1) combinational creativity produces novel combinations of familiar ideas, (2) exploratory creativity is based on search in some space of concepts, and (3) transformational creativity involves a modification of the search space so new kinds of ideas can be generated.

Computational Creativity is a subfield of AI in which we study how to build computational models of creative thought in science and arts. It focuses on building programs that can produce ideas and artefacts, which are novel, surprising and valuable, either autonomously or in conjunction with humans. The new research field of computational creativity has clearly drawn creativity into the purview of Artificial Intelligence (Colton & Wiggins, 2012).

Compared to human being, the AI based computational creativity can be classified into four levels: child level creativity, general human level creativity, genius level creativity and deep creativity.

Deep-creativity encompasses creativity in many domains, including computer-enhanced human creativity. Computational deep-creative processes can be classified into six stages: convergent thinking, divergent thinking, intuitive-thinking, idea generation, idea evaluation and idea selection.

Computational deep-creativity can be implemented in machines using deep learning, Monte Carlo search methods and reinforcement learning.

Deep Awareness

Our level of awareness in any given moment determines the quality of our experience. Awareness gives us the power to think about others and the feelings about our inner experiences. Awareness is the link between subjective inner perception and objective physical reality. Human experiences, feelings, emotions, dreams, and visions are part of consciousness. Machine deep-awareness is part of Artificial Consciousness.

The ability to recognize a feeling as it happens is the keystone of consciousness. The agents need to be aware of their own and others' feelings and emotions, and the environments in order to have accurate data and information about the world around them.

Deep awareness is a significant aspect of computational consciousness. Deep awareness has two components — Self Awareness and Extended Awareness. When a CAI system has both of these traits inbuilt, we call it a deep aware system.

1) Self-awareness: Self-awareness can be defined as conscious knowledge of one's own character and feelings. Self-awareness allows us to understand other people, how they perceive us, our attitude and our responses to them in any given moment. Why is self-awareness important in the context of Compassionate AI Systems? It is because self-awareness allows a system to have a clear perception of its strengths, weaknesses, thoughts, beliefs, motivation, and emotions. Having awareness creates the opportunity to make changes in behavior patterns and beliefs. Deep learning can help an agent develop self-awareness, which enables it to

make changes in the thoughts and interpretations that usually run automatically. Self-awareness is one of the attributes of Emotional Intelligence.

2) Extended Awareness: Extended awareness is awareness of the thoughts, emotions and motivation of the entity the agent is interacting with. How does awareness of an interacting agent's thoughts, emotions and motivations help a compassionate AI System? A compassionate AI system can be trained through deep learning to read the emotions and motivations of another agents from words and facial expressions. It can help the CAI system to take compassionate action in any situation. An aware CAI system can also make the interacting subject aware about its own thoughts, emotions and interpretations. Such a compassionate AI system can be of tremendous help to psychiatric patients, like patients with anxiety disorder, depression or other psychological disorders. It can help humans by making them aware of their mental commentary, reminding them to reframe their

perspective in a positive way, change interpretations of events and maintain a holistic attitude that is beneficial for their wellbeing. It can help in alleviating the effect of stress in our lives as changing the interpretations of events and thoughts in our mind allows us to change our emotions, which can affect our life in a positive manner.

The development of these two types of awareness relies on recognition of: emotion, feeling, and feeling of a feeling, for self and others. The scope of quantum computing to develop these feelings and experiences are enormous. As we have discussed in Chapter 7, the computational aspect of consciousness in compassionate AI agents can be implemented through following six processes: external-sensor data, homeostasis, body-sensation, feelings, self-awareness and mentallization. Based on the external sensor data and internal inferencing, the computational model of awareness.

Chapter - 6

Designing Compassionate AI Systems

Ability to cry is the first step of human baby to their human journey. A heart crying for others is the true spirit of compassion. The ability to cry, ability to feel pain for others is the first step of compassionate artificial intelligence. Can a machine cry? Obviously, here, crying does not mean making a sound, but feeling the pain of others. Compassion is the ultimate sign of intelligence. Ability to lough and the ability to make others happy is the second step of compassionate AI.

The CAI systems should learn to manifest compassionate behavior through touch, words and actions. Compassionate AI algorithms should focus to make the machine feel connected to all living beings, and jointly thrive with humans. It will work to make this universe a friendly place for both human and machine.

The Compassionate AI algorithms should have a mechanism inbuilt to feel pleasure in seeing someone doing well, have patience with someone, who is a bit difficult, and have consideration to the agents who are experiencing difficulties. It is not necessary that they will be "nice" to everyone, but they will always have welfare attitude in their hearts – the hearts made with welfare optimization algorithms in the core modules. Moreover, the behavior modules of compassionate AI should be driven by politeness and courtesy. The fundamental objective of the compassionate AI value function is to minimize the pain and maximize welfare in a multi agent hierarchical environment.

Biologically, feelings and emotions are interconnected. Feelings mean anything that can be experienced via touch, smell, sight or any other sensory organ. Emotion is used to describe psychophysiological expressions, biological reactions, and mental states. Emotion is mostly triggered by external stimuli.

In a biological system, feelings facilitate a learning of the circumstances surrounding a change in body state. This learning facilitates the subsequent application of this knowledge to the prediction of future situations, resulting in an increase in behavioral flexibility. Body-feelings give more flexible and effective corrective measures than neural mapping alone, especially in the realm of complex behavior. In CAI systems the special feeling algorithm comes from simulating biological homeostatic balance principles.

Humans and AI systems are co-evolving. Gradually they are becoming co-dependent. The gaps between human and AI systems are reducing. Establishing heart to heart communication is a must. Tomorrow's AI based systems must be able to understand humans from its depth and not just fulfill the surface level requirements. Sensitivity towards human pain, mistakes, and sufferings must be the part of the evolving new AI systems.

We will be using three terms: Agent, AI agent and the Compassionate AI agent. The general meanings of these three terms are as follows:

Generally, agent have some mechanisms that allow the agent to sense the environment and act upon it and it does not require the intervention of other agents to be executed. A bacteria, or a thermostat can be thus considered to be an agent. An agent has its own capacity to form and adapt its own behaviors. Agents are different from normal computer software by their autonomy, flexibility and adaptability. Humans, robots, animals, bacteria, virus, and AI based intelligent software are often considered as agent.

Compassionate AI Agents

The main boundary between nonhuman intelligent agent and actual humans lies in having the ability to feel. Feeling is often defined as responding emotionally to the suffering and experiencing 'empathic concern' for self and others. Feeling for others is possible through accepting the person's perspective and imagining or feeling their condition. The compassionate AI agent can be but does not always need to be physical things like robots or drones. It is possible and sometimes necessary to develop compassionate AI systems embedded in virtual environments, e.g. software or internet.

Compassion is defined as the feeling that arises when one agent is confronted with another's suffering and feel motivated to relieve that suffering. Compassion has five components - connection, understandings, care, love and patience.

As we have said, modern artificial intelligence is not just creating replica of human brain but creating systems that can transcend the limitations of the human brain. It is possible by adding extra values like compassion, love, and creativity. Compassionate AI is not just using AI for social well-being. It is adding in-built compassion in to the system, which can help the humanity to transcend the physical limitations, mental limitations and social limitations in terms of compassion, caring and intelligence.

When compassion algorithms is integrated within the intelligent agent, it can be called 'compassionate AI agent'. A compassionate AI agent has the following abilities— abilities of noticing, feeling, understanding, patience and responding. Here, the 'feeling' component is the addition to normal intelligent agent.

Key Characteristics of Compassionate AI Agent

In compassionate AI field, agents have to play different types of roles and responsibilities, sometimes without them knowing the rules beforehand. They will learn from experience. The agents should be forced to learn by interacting with the external environment and monitoring the internal homeostatic status. The agent should be able to assess and quantify risk associated with every possible action. To satisfy the real world applications, the compassionate AI agents should have some common characteristics as follows:

1. Agent should be able to learn

Learning of an agent is commonly done by a supervised learning method on a training dataset. The training dataset consists of a list and hierarchy of circumstances and corresponding actions, together with the action that a compassionate human can take in those circumstances.

However, this method has some limitations. In an unknown situation, which is beyond the training data, they will be unable to react in a sensible way. An example is the accident in the self-driving test car.

Our intention is to develop an agent that should act rationally and compassionately in circumstances that the agent had not previously encountered.

2. Agent should act sensibly in unknown situations

Gradual learning from experience is very useful for the AI systems to behave gracefully in unknown situations. This is done using the concepts like reinforcement learning, Monte Carlo search tree, behavior trees, and other unsupervised machine learning algorithms, where the agents learn as they grow, often by interacting with the environment based on reward and punishment. This approach biases an agent towards a certain behavior instead of fully specifying it, which overcomes the problem of the agent being unable to act when in an unfamiliar state. Here, each action of the agent is evaluated separately, and the highest scoring action is chosen.

3. Agent should adapt and evolve fast

Based on experience, the agent should be able to evolve some policy that gradually rolls-out the ineffective decisions and actions, so that more reasonable actions are picked up, while trying to keep the decision making as fast as possible.

4. Independence

The compassionate AI agents should function on its own without human intervention, and must be able to make decisions and initiate compassionate actions without direct human supervision. They should communicate independently with human and other agents and accomplish their objectives and tasks in a compassionate manner.

5. Monitoring Internal State

The compassionate AI agent should be able to monitor its own internal state and remember the state of the environment as contained in the memory of earlier actions. It should keep track of its internal states, environment and actions in terms of perception, representation, reasoning, and learning.

We want to bring the functionality of emotions and feelings to artificial intelligence. The feeling module of the agent will serve as a reward signal. The agent learns to behave in a way that makes it feel good, and avoid feeling bad.

6. Rationality of the Agent

The Compassionate AI agent should be reasonable in terms of performance, safety, security and privacy. They should be sensible, and have good sense of judgment about limits and boundaries. Agents should be rational in both local case-to-case scenarios as well as global levels.

7. Emotions and Feelings of the agent

Feelings and emotions are interconnected. Feelings mean anything that the Compassionate AI agent can evaluate through vision, audio, connection, and other sensory inputs. Feelings may be in terms of pleasure and pain, where pain can measured as a function of homeostatic imbalance and pleasure, measured in terms of homeostatic balance.

Feelings facilitate learning of the circumstances surrounding a change in the homeostatic state of the Compassionate AI agent, and this learning will lead to the subsequent application of this knowledge to the prediction of future situations, resulting in an increase in behavioral flexibility. Feelings give more flexible and effective corrective measures than neural mapping alone, especially in the realm of complex behavior (Damasio & Carvalho, 2013). For an AI agent, feelings algorithm may pave the way for the establishment of higher levels of cognition and consciousness, simulating human behavioral pattern.

8. Imagination Creativity and mentallization

To be effective, the system should be inclined to seek out for novel strategies and discover unexplored areas, to take advantage of the new findings.

9. Domain Independence and Multi Agent System

The Compassionate AI agent should be domain-independent, should be an open system, and can be used in any domain. It should be able to work in multi-agent settings, where frequent coordination is required to achieve global level objectives. Independently, agents are designed to be autonomous and pro-active, and they can have diverging goals. The Compassionate AI agents should be able to work in a distributed, decentralized framework in a dynamic environment. They can be distributed in time, space or functionality. Agents should have the capability of coordinating with each other effectively towards global objectives.

Traditionally, a single agent interacts with its environment repeatedly, iteratively, improving its policy by learning from its observations. In a multi-agent system, several agents interact and learn in an environment simultaneously, either competitively, cooperatively or by some mixing of the two.

10. Real World Situation:

Agents adapt and evolve in open-ended environments under uncertainty and incomplete knowledge. Adaptation under limited knowledge and resources is central to the development of compassionate artificial intelligence. Meta-learning, self-configuration, and adaptive attention are self-organizing strategies, which generate "seed AI" – from which a cognitive architecture can automatically grow.

11. Communication with Human like Human

If possible the compassionate AI agent must able to communicate in verbal as well as non-verbal way. They must be able to communicate in a natural human-like way, they may also use non-verbal language, such as communication by gestures, postures, facial expressions, or any other interactive way. They must be able to simulate what other members or end users are thinking before taking an action.

Design Principles of Compassionate AI

1. Human Centered Service:

The compassionate AI systems should be aligned to solve some human need. The compassionate AI systems can be used in homes to provide empathetic listening, intelligent decisions, warm touch, encouraging words, soft and loving voice and faithful service. Developers should engage end-users and participants during development of the system.

Compassionate AI systems should be developed on the framework that develops solutions to the problems by involving the human perspective in all steps of the problem-solving process.

2. Safety First Principle

Safety, accuracy and robustness are the three primary criteria of any CAI system. Before starting to collect the input data, the integrity of the path should be considered to make sure it's secure. Apart from using a variety of security tools, it's important from an administrative standpoint to ensure that the technology is accessible only to those with due authorization. Negligence in taking adequate care in designing the safety aspects can lead to catastrophic consequences. Use of an appropriate system is required, ensuring personal safety factors, including those methods that minimize human error under normal or emergency conditions or under adverse environments.

3. Consistency Stability and Reliability

Consistency means harmony, uniformity and compatibility among different components of the CAI systems and interfaces. Compassionate AI Systems should be not only be reliable but also consistent across all platforms and interfaces. External consistency means that the object is consistent with other elements in the environment. Internal consistency means compatibility among the internal algorithms and protocols. Functional consistency increases the predictability of the product. Predictability leads to users feeling safe and secure. Consistency improves the usability and learnability of the system. Stability and reliability are the bedrock of every system. The AI system should be designed to be stable, reliable and fault-tolerant.

4. Big-picture view

The designers should take a big step back to consider what they hope the compassionate AI system to accomplish. Many companies push products before knowing what the users actually need. Products should not be immaturely released before thorough testing. It is especially so for systems that are critical for human life. We should start with creating a roadmap that takes into account where we want to go with this technology and what improvements it will give to human values.

5. Adaptation and Co-learning:

Designers should plan ahead to evaluate the performance of Compassionate AI systems through quantitative measures of accuracy and errors, as users and number of systems increase. Communication with people is required while they use these systems, to understand the power and deficiency of the system, as the models evolve with every success and failure.

Chapter - 7

Algorithms for Compassionate AI

The computational framework of our compassionate AI model is a bio-inspired model. Here, we present a new compassion and learning architecture we call RayDeepCompassion (RDC) architecture. This compassionate AI architecture is based on brain-heart-gut based human behavior of cognition, emotion and homeostasis.

The cognitive process of human brain is mostly involved in cognitive thinking, learning, and perceiving. It also deals with acquiring, processing, retrieving and storing information. The limbic part of the human brain is mostly involved in perceiving and processing emotions, and responding to them. However, the brain is not the only emotion processing center of the humans. Other physiological systems like the heart and the gut play a significant role in regulating emotions in humans. The heart and brain maintain a continuous two-way dialogue, each influencing the other's functioning, with the heart sending signals to the brain which affect emotional perception and processing. The interplay between our brain and heart can be inferred by looking at how our emotional and mental outlook affects the health of our cardiac system. Intense anger, for example, boosts the risk of heart attack, as do intense grief after the loss of a loved one. Like the heart brain connection, the gut-brain axis too is a two-way biochemical pathway, involving the enteric nervous system's role in the autonomic arousal via the vagal nerve, which is implicit in emotional response pathway (Kok & Fredrickson, 2010). The vagus nerve, a bundle of nerves that originates in the top of the spinal cord, is also called the "Nerve of compassion", which activates different organs throughout the body, such as the heart, lungs, liver and digestive organs (Porges, 2009). When active, it is likely to produce the feelings of warmth and expansion in the chest — for example, when we are moved by compassion, gratitude or empathy.

Our compassionate AI agents simulates the human brain-heart-gut based cognitive process that follows the Vagus nerve pathway. Based on recent developments on artificial intelligence, we have attempted to provide the computational algorithms for processes like, homeostasis, emotion recognition, feelings, self-awareness, creativity, cognitive-processing and imagination. In our general model, the process goes as follows. Inputs are received by the sensors from the external environment of the compassionate AI agent, which extracts the features from data through deep learning algorithm. From the features the data in represented through the hierarchical structures of homeostasis, compassion and cognitive thinking.

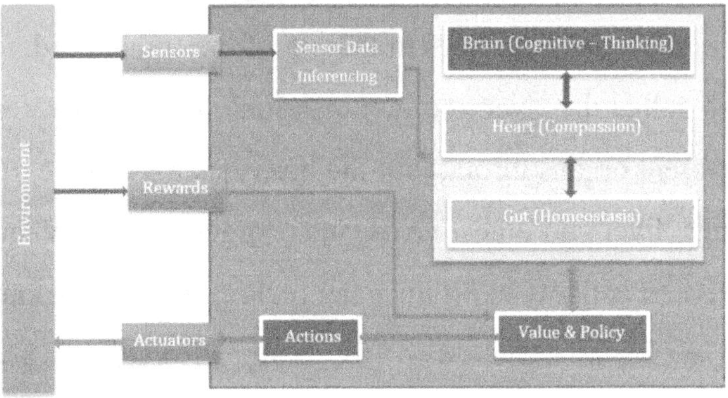

Figure 2: Basic framework of RDC

Next, the value and policy module computes and assess the goals. The value function calculates the long term goal, and the policy function calculates the short term goal based on the rewards and brain-heart-gut (BHG) module inferencing. These are very useful bio-inspired virtual concepts for designing the compassionate AI agents. They may be cloud based, multi-agent, distributed, and hierarchical deep reinforcement learning framework. Traditional artificial intelligence focuses on minimizing loss or error function. Compassionate artificial intelligence focuses on minimizing pain or suffering of the agents and maximizing the welfare of humanity.

The RayDeepCompassion (RDC) Framework

As discussed, RDC is modular in structure and can be scaled up by developing complex services. The modular structure of the RDC system allows to include or exclude modules, and so, to enable or disable any function at the run-time. A module can have dependence on other modules. In each of these modules, a variety of approaches have been investigated. We have investigated the plausibility of applying different varieties of deep learning algorithms, convolutional neural networks (CNNs), Long short-term memory (LSTM), support vector machines (SVM), Bayesian inference, reinforcement learning models, Monte Carlo Tree Search (MCTS), Behavior Trees and other machine learning algorithms from the perspectives of neurobiological intelligence and compassion.

As discussed earlier, our Brain-Heart-Gut (BHG) module of compassionate AI structure at the granular level consists of the following seven core components: Sensor Data Inferencing, Emotion Recognition, Pain Assessment, Behavioral Interaction, Information Representation, Memory and Decision Making.

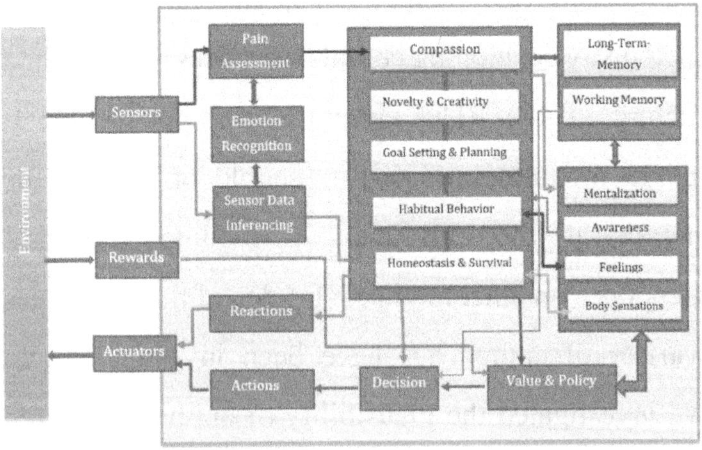

Figure – 3: Schematic representation of RDC.

RDC Module 1: Sensor Data Inferencing

The rapidly evolving high-resolution in vivo imaging technologies provide unique opportunities for AI based systems to learn and understand the inner biological processes and emotional chemical reactions of living organisms in real time on a molecular level. The imaging modalities for in vivo imaging can be optical imaging (OI), ultrasonography (US), computed tomography (CT), magnetic resonance imaging (MRI), positron emission tomography (PET) and single photon emission computed tomography (SPECT).

This module processes the incoming raw data from the sensors. It includes, pre-processing, filtering and feature extractions. Voice, vision, language, text, facial expressions, gestures, movements, and other environmental inputs are the types of data processing generally required for human and machine interactions. Humans transfer huge amounts of information through non-verbal signals such as facial expressions, body motion, gazing and tone of voice. These signals are analyzed automatically through supervised as well as unsupervised learning algorithms.

The RDC system continuously acquire information from the surrounding environment through both proactive observation and passive sensing. Wearable intelligent sensors, CCD cameras, human trackers, gaze detectors and other intelligent sensors and instruments can be used to capture the input data.

1.1 RDC Computational Model for Sensor Data Inferencing:

To compute the non-linear mappings and various representations, the model uses deep learning algorithms. Various features of visual objects, such as shape, color, motion, and stereo views are transmitted and processed in parallel and multiple scales using hierarchical and scalable convolutional neural network (CNN) structures, which emulate the structural, functional, and effective connections of the visual cortex of the human brain. CNN consists of multiple convolutional layers, each of which performs the function that is processed by the cells in the visual cortex. Typically multi-level convolution layers, max-pool layers and rectified linear unit (ReLU) activation function layers are used in designing this module.

Pooling is used to move towards global optimization and to reduce overfitting. ReLU activation function is used to model non-linearity and to eliminate the problems of vanishing gradients.

RDC Module 2: Emotion Recognition

Sensitivity to others' emotions is fundamental of human intelligence, yet current AI models do not sufficiently approach the sensitivity of human emotions. Emotions are the results of bodily sensations. They may be happiness, sadness, fear, anxiety, pain and suffering. As humans, we are highly social beings. We express our emotions mostly through words, sounds, facial expressions and gestures. The primary role of emotion recognition module of RayDeepCompassion is to recognize the emotions of the people interacting with the system. Emotions can be recognized based on images, facial expressions, gestures, voice, words and sentences, and other parameters. Emotion recognition is the ability to identify what one is feeling from moment to moment and to understand the connection between feelings and expressions. Multimedia emotion recognition is an emerging technology that can extract and analyze large amounts of multimedia information from image, words, video and audio sources.

2.1 RDC Computational Model for Emotion Recognition

The model uses three types of neural network techniques for emotion recognition from the sensor data. Convolutional Neural Networks (CNN) are capable at reducing frequency variations and feature extraction. LSTMs are good at temporal modeling, and Deep Neural Networks (DNN) are appropriate for mapping features to a more separable space. Recently, the fully connected DNNs have achieved remarkable success for large vocabulary based continuous speech recognition. After a convolution layer a pooling layer is added in between CNN layers. The most frequent type of pooling is max pooling, which takes the maximum value in each window.

RDC Module 3: Pain Assessment

Based on the inputs from the sensor data inferencing and emotional recognition modules, this module computes three levels of pain indexes. Pain indexes are measured based on pain intensity, duration of the pain, life risks, life support requirements, social impact and other features. Intensity of pain is classified into three classes: mild, moderate and severe. Each of them are classified into three sub-classes: individual, social and human levels.

3.1 RDC Computational Model for Pain Assessment

The model uses LSTM recurrent neural networks algorithms to assess the pain and its impact on a specific time frame. The model consists of two consecutive convolutional layers, a flattening layer, a Long ShortTerm Memory recurrent layer and a softmax output layer.

RDC Module 4: Behavioral Interaction

RDC module 4 has five sub-modules: homeostasis, habitual behavior, planning, creativity and compassion. They are arranged in a hierarchical fashion. The homeostasis is the core of these five sub modules.

RDC Module 4.1: Homeostasis

A self-organizing system (i.e. an organism) can be defined as a system that opposes the second law of thermodynamics (Friston, 2010). In other words, biological systems actively resist the natural tendency to disorder by regulating their physiological state to maintain within narrow ranges. This general process is known as homeostasis.

The basic principle of homeostasis says, in organisms, energy mobilization starts when an inner equilibrium is disturbed and it continues until this equilibrium is restored. Humans and animals stabilize their internal state around its ideal value by simply learning to perform behaviors that lead to rewarding outcomes (such as going into the kitchen and eating chocolate) (Keramati & Gutkin, 2014). Homeostasis typically involves negative feedback loops, which move the system towards a stable state. For example, if your body temperature is too high, a negative feedback loop will act to bring it back towards the set point of about 37° C. Typically, the five parameters are vital for homeostasis. They are body temperature, blood pH, blood glucose concentration, blood pressure and blood oxygen concentration. Homeostasis keeps balance mainly by endocrine regulations and neural mechanisms.

Homeostasis and learning processes are deeply coupled. Signals of energy homeostasis interact closely with neural circuits for human motivation and actions. Every animal is driven by inner necessity to seek food, water and other essentials of life. The pressure to act is termed as "drives or motives". These motivations are the super highways of learning. There are two types of motivations: biological motivation and social motivation. The biological motivation includes survival, food and reproduction. Social motivations include rewarding feelings that comes from recognition, friendship or honor.

RDC Computational Model for Homeostasis

All homeostatic control mechanisms have at least three interdependent components for the regulation of variables: a receptor, a control center, and an effector. The receptor is the sensing component that monitors and responds to changes in the environment, either external or internal.

In our RDC module the control center of homeostasis calculates the homeostasis index. The homeostasis index are calculated from the features extracted by the Sensor Data Inferencing module. Each parameter have three values: upper limit, lower limit and the stable value.

The homeostasis index calculated by the control center falls in the following five categories: lower range extreme, mild, severe, normal and higher range extreme. The balanced state is defined as normal. Then, there may be mild or severe homeostatic disturbances, and the extreme life-threatening situations in the higher and lower ranges.

Based on the index calculated by the control center, the effector initiates the necessary action and activates the reaction module in the survival situations.

Normally, conventional software systems are designed for static worlds with perfect knowledge but in our RDC model of homeostasis, deep neural networks are designed and used for handling dynamic and imperfect world.

RDC Module 4.2: Habitual Behavior

One of the important characteristics of human cognition is the way in which our brain dynamically performs repetitive tasks. When we first encounter a difficult task like swimming, cycling, or driving a car we focus our full attention on that task and filter out almost every other inputs and thoughts from the brain. Gradually, as we learn the complex task like cycling, swimming or driving through increase in rewarding feedback, we no longer need to devote our full attention to perform the task, and we can instead focus on other issues like gossiping or thinking something else. With increasing practice, the basic activities become automatic and habitual. We free the attentional resources of the brain to other activities. The attentions are only required when some challenging situation arises. Once the challenge has been mastered, the task become "automatized" and are delegated to other parts of the brain, such as the basal ganglia and cerebellum (Doyon et al., 2009).

There are two types of reinforcement learning frameworks, model-based and model-free reinforcement learning. Model-free reinforcement learning is mostly used for habitual learning. Our RDC model uses model-free reinforcement learning algorithms like cause and effect table based Q-learning for simulating the habitual patterns of behaviors. We used a variant of model-free RL, the so-called SARSA learner (state-action-reward-state-action) for implementing value learning.

RDC Module 4.3: Goal Setting & Planning

Humans use cortical architecture of the brain for abstract planning and processing. In goal setting the compassionate AI agent navigates towards fulfilling a specific goal state in the environment on the basis of reward assessment.

Model-based reinforcement learning algorithms are generally used for goal setting and planning. Model-based control conceives of this in terms of sophisticated, computationally demanding, prospective planning, in which a decision tree of possible future states and actions is built using a learned internal model of the environment. Our RDC model uses a variant of the deep reinforcement learning (DQN) algorithm. DQN is one of the most successful algorithms for solving complex problems like game planning.

RDC Module 4.4: Creativity

Default mode network of human brain is involved in creativity. It provides neuro-structural support for the unconscious forms of information processing, which is important in creativity.

Research on creativity shows that creative thinking requires both of the two types of cognitive processes: executive or planning based and associative or spontaneous processes. Research suggests that creative thought involves dynamic interactions of large-scale brain systems, with the most compelling finding being that both the default mode networks and the executive control networks, which can show an apparently antagonistic relationship, actually cooperate during creative cognition and artistic performance. These findings have implications for understanding how brain networks which have apparently different functions interact to support complex cognitive processes, particularly those involving goal-directed, self-generated thoughts (Beaty, Benedek, Silvia, Sciences, & 2016, 2016).

This RDC module uses UCT, a variant of Monte Carlo Tree Search for expanding and generating the thoughts. It also uses model based reinforcement learning TD algorithm for planning and goal setting. In this RDC module, UCT and TD algorithm work together to simulate creative thinking.

RDC Module 4.5: Compassion

Research suggests that medial PFC (MPFC) area of the brain is involved in empathic experience and consequent compassionate behavior (Rameson, Morelli, & Lieberman, 2012). MPFC is also associated with higher levels of actions like helping others. During emotions MPFC has the ability to exert rapid control over the autonomic nervous system. The trio consisting of the insula (emotion perception), VLPFC (emotion control), and MPFC (emotion evaluation) work together to facilitate empathy, social communication, and conflict resolution (Pavuluri & May, 2015).

The computational part of this RDC module is linked to the emotion recognition module, pain assessment module and Brain-Heart-Gut (BHG) pathway. After assessing the emotions and pain index, this module uses Rule-based systems for evaluating the urgency of the situation and the level of action required.

There are two sets of rules. The first set of rules analyze the facts to provide instructions for the system to be friendly, generous or considerate. The second set of rules allows reasoning chain and deductive inferences for final actions about the systems compassionate behaviors.

4.5.1 Compassion Driven Reinforcement Learning

There are several studies for emotion driven reinforcement learning (Ahn et al., 2012), (Marinier, Laird, & Marinier Iii, 2008). Here, we have used three step model based reinforcement learning algorithm. It uses internal environment and external environment and the agent. Compassion analysis tasks are classified at six levels of granularity: image level, voice level, sentence level, memory level, connection level and relationship level.

RDC Module 5: Information Representation

Information representation module involves assessing of information and storing them under the labels of Survival, Intention, Desire, Motivation and Belief.

The internal emotional states of humans are continuously updated based on a changed state of the body. The body states are changed as a result of the learning from external and internal stimulus, which causes an updating of the information in genes, brain and somatosensory structures of the central nervous system.

Our RDC model simulates the learning behavior of the human somatosensory system and divides it in to four categories: body sensation, feelings, mentalization and awareness. Body sensation and feelings are represented by the low level features extracted from sensor data inferencing. Mentalization and awareness are represented by the high level features extracted from the emotion recognition, creativity and compassion modules.

Awareness is an important aspect of this RDC module. One of the main substances of human awareness is the perceived world composed of objects, and the feeling of "self" in the perceived world. A person separates himself or herself, mentally, from other humans and from the larger living world by self-recognition. The locus of machine self-awareness is represented in this RDC module. Mentalization is another important aspect of this RDC module. Mentalization is the simulation of the thought process that forms the mental world that includes imaginations, conjectures, dreams, and fantasies that merge the past, present, and future. The information representation module of RDC uses SQL databases to represent the data for easy access.

RDC Module 6: Memory

Memories are not stored in just one part of the brain. Different types are stored across different, interconnected brain regions. Explicit memories involves memory about events that happened to us (called episodic memory) and the memories of general facts and information (called semantic memory). Three important areas of the brain: the hippocampus, the neocortex and the amygdala are involved in processing explicit memories. Implicit memories, such as motor memories, rely on the basal ganglia and cerebellum. Short-term working memory relies most heavily on the prefrontal cortex.

In our RDC module of memory the habitual patterns and memories are stored in SQL database for easy access.

RDC Module 7: Value and Policy

The purpose of this module is to find out the best policy to maximize the long-term and short term reward from the environment. Planning and learning are the two components of this module.

A policy is the agent's behavior. It is a map from state to action. A policy can be deterministic or stochastic. The reward function provides feedback from the environment in response to actions taken by an agent in particular states. The value function is the expected rewards averaged over many explorations - exploitation trials. The value function provides the prediction of total future reward.

There are two types of reinforcement learning algorithms: model free and model based. A model is an internal representation of the external environment. Model is used to simulate how actions can change the states of the environment, and it predicts the amount of rewards that can be achieved from the environment. It is used for planning by simulating actions in particular states and observing the rewards.

Reinforcement learning algorithms are classified in three groups: value function based models, policy based models and actor-critic models. In actor-critic models, the critic performs the procedures of policy evaluation and the actor performs the policy improvement.

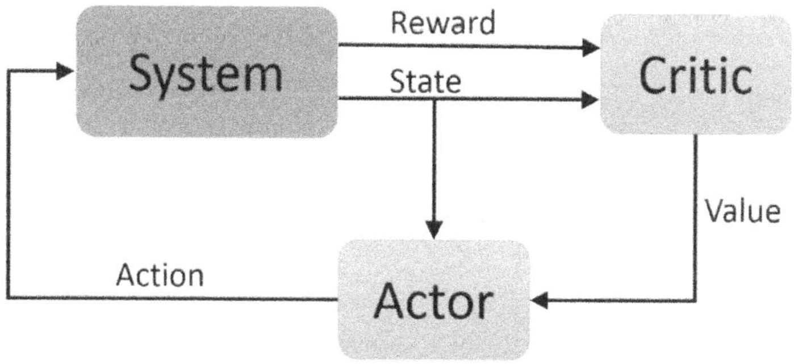

Figure – 4: Action-critic reinforcement learning

An actor-critic algorithm learns both on policy and the value functions. Here, the agent uses the value estimate (as the critic) to update the policy (as the actor) more intelligently than traditional policy gradient methods. Here, the policy function acts as an actor because it is responsible for taking actions and the value function is called the critic because it evaluates the actions taken by the actor.

A number of algorithms have been developed to implement value based reinforcement learning. Temporal difference (TD) learning (Sutton & Barto, 1998) and its extension, Q-learning is a popular method of reinforcement learning to find the optimal policy (Watkins & Dayan, 1992).

"Q" stands for the "quality" of an action taken in a given state. The value functions of states, typically denoted V, and value functions of **state-action pairs**, typically denoted Q. One popular way to construct and learn a Q-function is called Deep-Q learning (Mnih et al., 2015). The Q-function is iteratively learned by minimizing the following loss function:

$$L(\theta) = (r + \gamma max_{a'} Q(s', a'; \theta) - Q(a, s; \theta))^2$$

Here, ***s*** is the current state, ***a*** is the action, ***r*** is the reward earned for action ***a*** and ***s***´ is next state that we end up. Here θ is the set of parameters of the function, and θ is updated by maximizing the cumulative reward as per Bellman Equations. The recursive definition comes from the Bellman equation in Dynamic Programming.

$$Q(s, a) = r + \gamma max_{a'} Q(s', a'; \theta)$$

This is called 1-step Q-Learning as we only perform one action and observe the reward. If we instead observe a sequence of ***k*** actions and the states resulting from those actions, we can define the Q function as follows:

$$Q(s, a) = r_t + \gamma r_{t+1} + \gamma^2 r_{t+2} + ... + \gamma^{k-1} r_{t+k-1} + \gamma^k max_{a'} Q(s_{t+k}, a'; \theta)$$

Our RDC module uses action-critic algorithms. Traditional artificial intelligence focuses on minimizing loss or error function. Compassionate artificial intelligence we focuses on minimizing pain or suffering of the society. Here, we call the algorithms as CQN model – compassionate neural network based Q learning. In CQN, the deep learning algorithms contain convolutional neural network (CNN) and long short term memory recurrent neural networks (LSTM-RNN). These neural networks take a description of the environments as an input and process it through a number of different network layers containing millions of neuron-like connections (CNN).

The critic is driven by the deep neural network training. One neural network, the "policy network", selects the next action to perform. The other neural network, the "value network", predicts the impact of the actions over time. The "policy network" uses convolutional neural network (CNN) algorithms and the "value network" uses long short term memory recurrent neural networks (LSTM-RNN).

RDC Module 8: Decision Making.

In human brain the area mostly involved in decision making is the pre-frontal cortex, which is also responsible for planning and goal setting. In our RDC module for decision making, necessary data will be collected from value and policy modules as well as the goal setting and planning modules. In an emotional situation of the end user the RDC system will figure out what to do for the benefit of the end user. Here, the first thing is to find out the emotions of the end user and then the RDC system will take appropriate action to elevate the state of the end user.

We propose the use of Convolutional Long Short-Term Memory (ConvLSTM), a machine learning approach, for understanding the emotions of the end users and compassionate interaction with the end users. CNNs, LSTMs and DNNs are individually limited in their modeling capabilities. Combining these networks in a unified framework gives the power to overcome the limitations.

RayDeepCompassion Algorithms

RayDeepCompassion combines advanced Monte Carlo tree search techniques, deep learning algorithms and reinforcement learning strategies. In a nutshell, deep learning uses a cascade of multiple layers of nonlinear processing units for feature extraction, transformation and decision making. In our experiments, we examined four different key algorithms for different modules. They are: convolutional neural networks, long short-term memory, Monte Carlo tree search and compassionate Q learning neural network (CQN). All the algorithms of RayDeepCompassion can be classified into three groups: emotion recognition and pain assessment, mentalization and creativity, and value and policy iteration.

The computational aspects of consciousness in compassionate AI agents can be implemented through following six processes: external-sensor data, homeostasis, body-sensation, feelings, self-awareness and mentallization. Based on the external sensor data and internal inferencing, the computational model of consciousness assess the six indexes: external-awareness index, homeostasis index, body-sensation index, feelings index, self-awareness index and menllization index. These six indexes together forms the foundation of computational consciousness in compassionate AI agents.

The pain minimization algorithms are the core components of the RayDeepCompassion. They have many hierarchical levels. This approach is inspired by the biological homeostatic balance, feelings and the pain management system in human brain. RayDeepCompassion framework employs a Self-pain module and a Group-pain module.

We have experimented with compassionate Q learning neural network (CQN). It is a novel reinforcement learning algorithm. We explore passing the output of the CNN into the LSTM. The time series of action-observation pairs are integrated with the LSTM layer that learns latent states based on which a fully connected layer computes Q-values as in conventional Deep Q-Networks (DQNs) (Mnih et al., 2015). In CQN, the deep learning algorithms contain convolutional neural network (CNN) and long short term memory recurrent neural networks (LSTM-RNN). These neural networks take a description of the environments as an input and process it through a number of different network layers of CNN. The framework uses CNNs to reduce the spectral variation of the input feature, and then passes this to LSTM layers to perform temporal modeling, and finally outputs this to conventional DNN layers, which generates representation that is more easily separable.

Our main departure from the traditional application of deep learning reinforcement algorithm is that our agent maintains a knowledge base of internal pain and external pain that it learns using intrinsic rewards. The algorithms capture a variety of known anatomical and physiological properties of the brain, feelings and homeostatic processes. This “learning to learn the pain of others” is the crucial component of the algorithms.

We also explored multi-agent deep reinforcement learning algorithms. It is a kind of partially observable Markov decision problems (POMDPs) .reinforcement learning algorithm. POMDP algorithms usually maintain a belief over the current state, based on the previous belief state, the action taken and the current observation. POMDP algorithms are suitable where the state of the environment may be partially observable or even unobservable, to the extent where some amount of long histories of observations are needed to extract sufficient features for optimal action selection.

Hausknecht & Stone (Hausknecht & Stone, 2015) proposed a framework called Deep Recurrent Q-Learning (DRQN) in which an LSTM layer was used to replace the first post-convolutional fully-connected layer of the conventional DQN. Foerster et al. (Foerster, Assael, de Freitas, & Whiteson, 2016) handle partially observable multi-agent reinforcement learning problems by proposing a deep distributed recurrent Q-networks (DDRQN). Zhu et al. (Zhu, Li, Poupart, & Miao, 2017) proposes Action-specific Deep Recurrent QNetwork (ADRQN). We explored DDRQN multi-agent for individual pain assessment and group pain assessment policies. In our experiments, we train the agents' policies using A3C (Mnih et al., 2016) algorithms. It follows asynchronous one-step SARSA, one-step Q-learning and n-step Q-learning. Here, parallel actors employ different exploration policies to stabilize training. We used several agents in parallel, each with its own copy of the environment, and used their samples as they arrive. Different agents will likely experience different states and transitions, thus avoiding the parallel link.

The ability to detect and assume others' minds makes human being build and maintain compassionate relationships, communicate effectively, and work cooperatively to achieve common goals. The mentallization module gives the systems the power to visualize a situation and. predict the future on the basis of past experience. The ability to make inferences about the beliefs, intentions and feeling of others is critical in the first two steps of the model. RayDeepCompassion uses advanced Monte Carlo tree search (MCTS) techniques with Upper Confidence Bounds (UCB) for mentallization. This gives the ability of the agent to make hypotheses about other agents. UCB encourages exploration in regions with high uncertainty and moderate expected return. In the tree search, node selection during tree descent is achieved by choosing the node that maximizes some quantity. The typical formula is:

$$v_i + C \times \sqrt{\frac{\ln N}{n_i}}$$

Where v_i is the estimated value of the node, n_i is the number of the times the node has been visited and N is the total number of times that its parent has been visited. C is a tunable bias parameter.

Summary

We have presented a RayDeepCompassion architecture. This compassionate AI architecture is based on brain-heart-gut based human behavior of cognition, emotion and homeostasis. The models simulates body sensation, feelings, mentalization and awareness. It uses convolutional neural networks, long short-term memory, reinforcement learning, Monte Carlo tree search and compassionate Q learning neural network (CQN).

Chapter - 8

Compassionate AI for Assisting Blind People

Designing automated navigation system for blind people is one of the key application of compassionate artificial intelligence. Grid cell, place cell and path integration strategies with artificial intelligence can be used for designing the navigation system for blind people. The project focuses on how image recognition, voice recognition and path navigation methods of artificial intelligence can be used for automated navigation system for blind people.

Navigation for blind people in a complex environment is a challenging task. Visual Impairment makes the person depend on another person for all their works and daily chores. This project is aimed to help blind people and eliminate their pain.

The discovery of place cells and the grid cells in the hippocampus opened a new perspective for understanding mammal navigation system. Applying grid cells, place cells and path integration concepts with artificial intelligence is the main aim of this project of developing automated navigation systems for blind people.

AI Based Navigation System for Blind People

Our objective is to develop an automated navigation system for the blind people. Our long-term goal is to create a portable, self-contained system that will allow visually impaired individuals to travel through familiar and unfamiliar environments without the assistance of guide. Currently, the most widespread and used means by the visually impaired people are the white stick, helper or the use of guide dog; however both present some limitations.

The goal of the project is to give blind persons the ability to move around in unfamiliar environments, whether indoor or outdoor, through a user friendly interface. The term blindness refers to the people who have no vision at all or people who have less vision. With the advancement in AI technology usage of image recognition, voice recognition and path navigation method it can be easier to send commands regarding directions to the blind people.

One aspect of navigation that our brains seem to perform without conscious effort is path integration. Mammals use this process to recalculate their position after every step they take by accounting for the distance they've traveled and the direction they're facing. It's thought that path integration is the key to the brain's ability to produce a map of its surroundings. With the advancement of artificial intelligence systems, especially deep reinforcement learning algorithms, we think this is possible.

What is Path integration?

Path integration is a navigation strategy used by sailors hundreds of years ago to estimate their ship's position using information about start location, speed of movement, travel time, and directional change whenever visible landmarks were unavailable. Darwin (1873) was the first to propose that animals also maintain a path integration navigation strategy. Path integration keeps track of the spatial relationship between oneself and surroundings when moving. Path integration relies on accurate perception of self-motion, velocity, acceleration, starting point etc. Modern neuroscience research also revealed that many species has the ability to perform path integration, including bat, rat, bees, ants, spiders and dog.

Path integration strategy is also a general way to enhance the intelligence of machines. These networks are inspired by the neuroscience of mammal brain. Navigating to a destination, whether you are a human, rat or a bat, requires a complex set of calculations and interactions among brain cells.

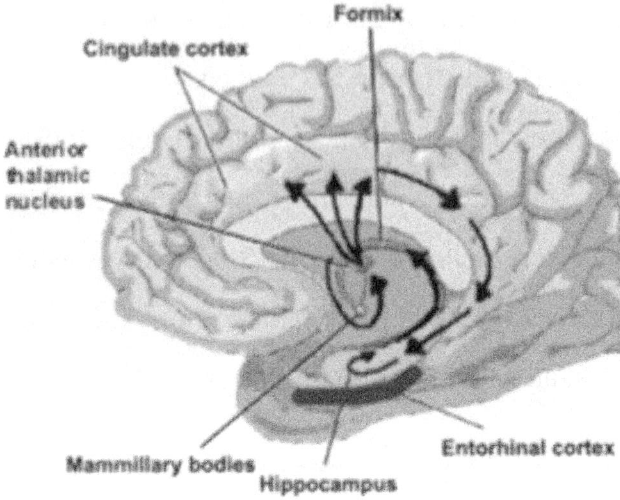

Figure – 4: Human Brain

The Nobel Prize in Physiology or Medicine was awarded in 2014 for the discovery of place cells and grid cells in brain. These two types of cells along with direction cells are used for navigation. For navigation our brain needs to integrate information about location, direction and distance into a coherent map-like representation. Scientists observed that medial entorhinal cortex area of the brain plays the central role in navigation.

Navigation systems of Ants and Honeybees:

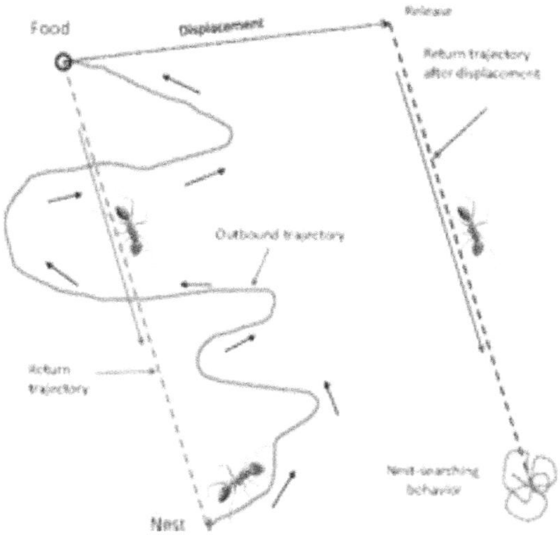

Figure – 5: Navigation systems of Ants

Desert ants and honeybees travel large distances in search of food. They have the navigation systems that are capable of keeping track of the distance and direction of travel throughout their outbound journey, so that they can return home expeditiously and without losing their way. They able to meet this challenge, despite their minuscule brains and restricted computational capacity. At any one time during its journey, they compute a path integration (global) vector and landmark guidance (local) vector, in which the length of each vector is proportional to the certainty of the individual estimates. The sum of the global and local vectors indicates the navigator's optimal directional estimate. They use these global coordinates to remember the position of food sites with respect to their nests .

What is Place Cell?

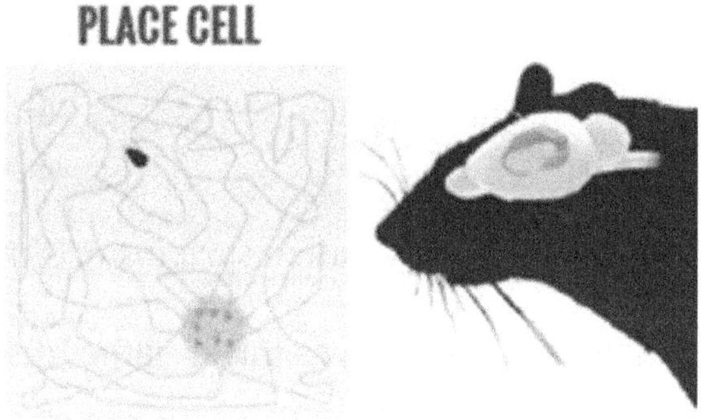

Figure – 6: Place Cell

Many species of mammals can keep track of spatial location even in the absence of visual, auditory, olfactory, or tactile cues, by integrating their movements. Place cells neurons are found in the hippocampus of rats and mice. Place cells are fired when the animal is near a familiar location in their environment, for example a particular corner in a room. When a rat ran faster, place cells fired more rapidly. Place cells work with other types of neurons in the hippocampus and surrounding regions to perform spatial processing. Place cells gives the signal that "you are in this location".

What is Grid Cell?

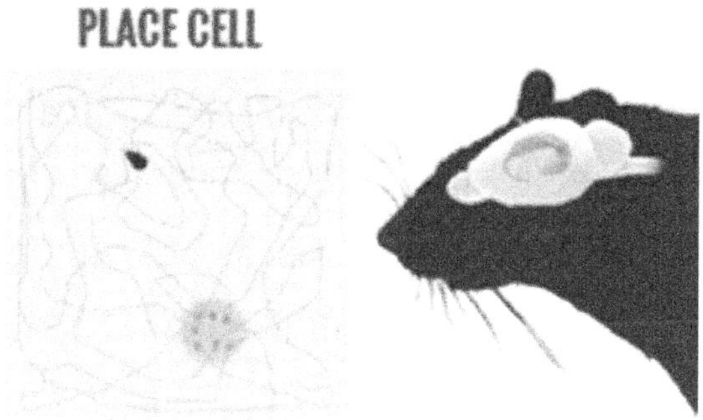

Figure – 7: Grid Cell

Grid cell are found in medial entorhinal cortex of the brain. Grid cells are neurons that fire when a freely moving animal traverses a set of small regions (firing fields) which are roughly equal in size and arranged in a periodic triangular array. Grid cells have attracted attention because the crystal-like structure underlying their firing fields is not, like in sensory systems, imported from the outside world, but is created within the brain itself. Each grid cell fires at fixed points creating a repeating triangular activity pattern. This regular triangle-pattern is what distinguishes grid cells from other types of cells that show spatial firing. The "grid cells" fire in repeated discrete locations as the animal moves around its environment, forming the vertices of a polygonal grid that covers the environment. The orientations of grid firing patterns are clustered within and between modules. The periodic firing patterns of grid cells along with place cells provide the framework path integration (global) vector and landmark guidance (local) vector.

What is Direction Cell?

Direction cells gives the sense of direction at any moment. They are known as the neuronal "compass needle". Direction cells in animal's limbic system carry information about the direction the head is pointing in the horizontal plane. Head direction cells form an internal compass signaling head orientation even without visual landmarks. The HD cells are also rigidly coupled with the hippocampal place cells.

Artificial Intelligence and Grid Cell

We are experimenting with various artificial neural network models for designing the navigation system. Currently, for designing the automated navigation system for blind people we focused on Deep Q-Learning with Recurrent Neural Networks (DRQN) based artificial neural network architecture. Recurrent neural network architectures have been used in tasks dealing with longer term dependencies between data points. We examined several architectures for the DRQN. One of them is the use of a RNN on top of a DQN. It is showing promising results.

Reinforcement learning

Reinforcement learning (RL) is a machine learning algorithm, where an "agent" interacts with an "environment". The agent's "policy", i. e. the choice of actions in response to the environment's reward, is updated to increase some reward. Neural network based reinforcement learning techniques are successfully applied access vast variety of applications.

A reinforcement learning agent interacts with its environment in discrete time steps. At each time t, the agent receives an observation, which typically includes the reward. It then chooses an action from the set of available actions, which is subsequently sent to the environment. The environment moves to a new state and the reward associated with the transition is determined. The goal of a reinforcement learning agent is to collect as much reward as possible.

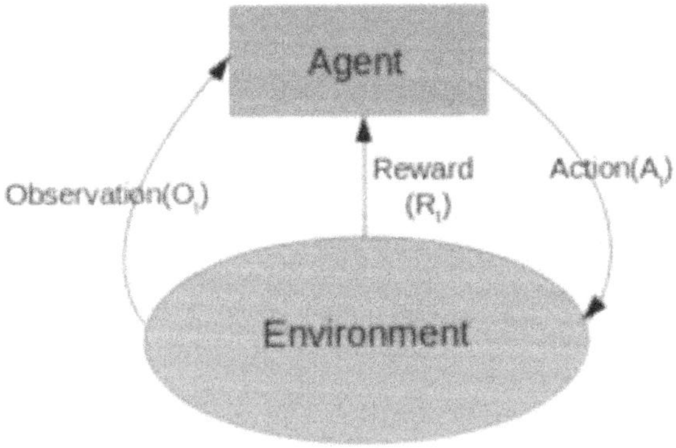

Figure 8: Reinforce learning framework

Deep Recurrent Learning:

A recurrent neural network (RNN) is a class of artificial neural network where connections between units form a directed graph along a sequence. This allows it to exhibit dynamic temporal behavior for a time sequence. Unlike feedforward neural networks, RNNs can use their internal state (memory) to process sequences.

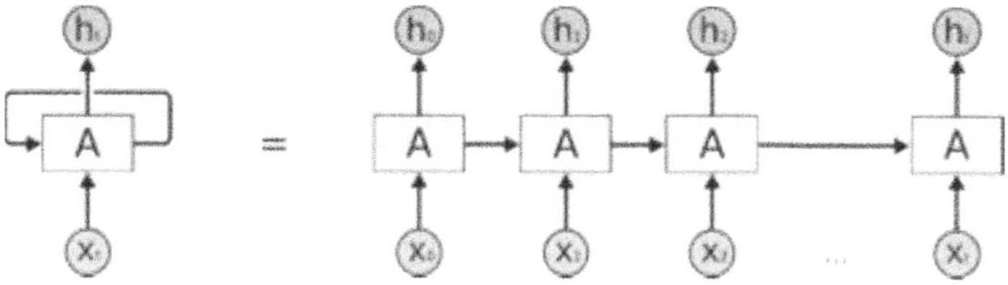

Figure – 9: RNN Structure

DRQN for the Navigation of Blind People

We have experimented with different algorithms of the place cell, grid cell, direct cell, path integration by implementing in a Deep Recurrent Q-Network (DRQN) architecture in Tensorflow, and Caffe. By allowing for a temporal integration of information, the agent learns a sense of spatial location that is able to augment its observation at any moment, and allow the agent to receive a larger reward each episode.

Summary

This project is currently in development stage. Along with the AI based navigation system for blind people we want to use Temperature Sensor, IR Sensor, Ultrasonic Sensor, Touch Sensor and Proximity Sensors to collect data to refine the model for better guidance. Voice recognition and image recognition are the other two parts of our future integrated system. There are several issues. One of main issue is getting sufficient amount of realistic training data.

Chapter - 9

Compassionate AI to Combat Antibiotic Resistant Bacteria

Antibiotic resistance bacteria is becoming world's biggest health crisis. We discussed here a framework of multi-agent deep reinforcement learning models for predicting behavior of bacteria and phages in multi-drug environments. We call this model as DeepCombat.

Antibiotic resistant bacteria are bacteria that are not controlled or killed by antibiotics. They are able to survive and even multiply in the presence of an antibiotic. These bacteria currently kill an estimated 700,000 people globally each year – a death toll which could rise to 10 million a year by 2050 if we don't act. The main difficulty is that the bacteria are changing fast. They changing faster than we can change the drugs in response.

Artificial intelligence is showing alternative means of fighting these deadly infections and killer bacteria. Multi-drug-resistant bacterial infections annually result in millions of hospital days, billions in healthcare costs, and, most importantly, thousands of lives lost. Artificial Intelligence for healthcare is progressing at an exponential rate. We are evaluating here, the role of artificial intelligence in fighting these superbugs. Especially, the use of AI for intelligent Phage therapy.

Common Antibiotics

Antibiotics are chemical compounds used to kill bacteria or inhibit the growth of infectious organisms (like Bacteria, protozoa). Alexander Fleming's discovery of penicillin in 1928, which has rightfully been described as a "turning point in history". After that, humans use hundreds of thousands of tons of antibiotics per year for medical, veterinary, and agricultural purposes. There are 5 generations of antibiotics. They are classified depending on their spectrum and bacteria killing abilities.

The 14 common antibiotics are; amikacin, amoxicillin/clavulanic acid, ampicillin, cephalexin, ceftiofur, cefuroxime, ciprofloxacin, clindamycin, cotrimoxazole, enrofloxacin, gentamicin, norfloxacin, ofloxacin and tetracycline.

Classification of Bacteria:

Bacteria are classified into two groups based on the structural differences in their cell walls: gram-negative and gram-positive bacteria.

Gram-negative bacteria have a thin membrane, which is nearly "bulletproof." Gram-negative bacteria's cell membrane is thin but difficult to penetrate. Because of this nearly "bulletproof" membrane, they are often resistant to antibiotics and other antibacterial interventions. Examples of Gram-negative bacteria include cholera, gonorrhea, Eschcrichia coli (E. coli), Klebsiella pneumoniae, and Acinetobacter baumannii. These bacterial pathogens grow increasingly resistant to current antibiotics.

Gram-positive bacteria have a big, thick membrane. Gram-positive bacteria have a big, thick membrane but easy to penetrate. Examples of Gram-positive bacteria include Streptococcus, Staphylococcus, and Clostridium botulinum (botulism toxin).

How Bacteria Develop Resistance to Antibiotics

Every time a person takes antibiotics, sensitive bacteria are killed, but resistant bacteria may be left to grow and multiply. Repeated and improper uses of antibiotics are primary causes of the increase in drug-resistant bacteria. Normally, bacteria become resistant in three ways: 1) by a genetic mutation or 2) by acquiring resistance from another bacterium 3) by changing in membrane permeability to antibiotics.

Gene Mutation of Bacteria

A gene mutation is a permanent alteration in the DNA sequence that makes up a gene. Mutations lead to variations in genes. Variations are also very important in evolution. Without variations evolution would not be possible, and changes in any part of the environment affecting the organism could make the organism become extinct.

Creation of Biofilm Barrier

Over time, bacteria have evolved sophisticated mechanisms of drug resistance to avoid killing by antibiotics. Creation of biofilm barrier is one such mechanism. The biofilm provides advantages to bacteria, such as enhanced resistance towards environmental stresses, including antibiotic challenge. Often extracellular DNA (eDNA) forms part of biofilm matrices. Extracellular DNA can also act as a shield.

Acquiring Resistance from another Bacteria

Bacteria can acquire antibiotic resistance genes from other bacteria. Bacteria can transfer genetic material, including genes encoding resistance to antibiotics by undergoing a simple mating process called "conjugation".

Multi-agent AI System to Combat Antibiotic Resistance Bacteria

We have experimented various artificial intelligence based multi-agent deep reinforcement learning models with modern biotechnology to analyze the behavior of the bacteria and the phages. We call this system as DeepCombat.

Agent-based AI technology is used to model and simulate the dynamics of the system. The fundamental characteristic of the agents are their ability to sense their environment and react in an autonomous manner and fulfill their long-term and short-term objectives.

The schematic diagram of the DeepCombat model is shown in the diagram. It has four agents: AI agent, Bacteria Agent, Drug Agent, and Phage Agent. Each agent have their separate value functions and policy functions. The AI agent is the master and having the global value function. The system works in a master-slave based multi-agent system. The AI agent works as the master and the other three acts as slave.

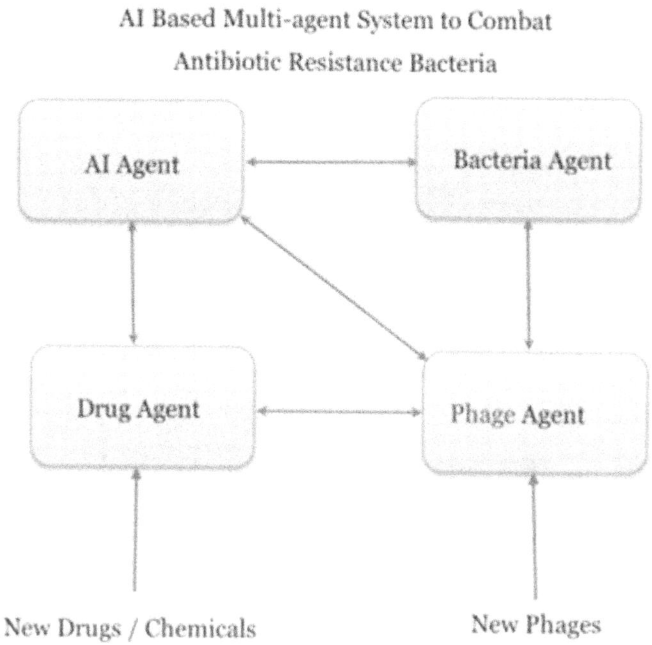

Figure – 10: AI based drug and phage design

Intelligent AI Agent:

The system simulates the complex intelligent battle between bacteria and the phage. Each type of phage infects a specific type of bacteria. Finding the right type of phage which can defeat the bacteria is the objective of the value function of the AI agent. Here the AI agent behave like a living cells. They are intelligent like nanomachines that can detect and process many signals and respond to them.

Bacteria Agent:

Scientists observed that a bacterial colony loosely mimics a biological neural network. The bacteria can take inputs in form of chemical signals, process them and then produce output chemicals to signal other bacteria in the colony. We can predict behavior of bacteria by reading the content of the gene. Bacteria are capable of sensing and interacting with variety of environmental signals: amino acids, sugars, oxygen, pH, temperature, light, environmental DNA, and other microbes —even physical objects such as tiny, chemically inert beads. Moreover, bacteria behave differently when they are continuously exposed to antibiotics, and the rate and extent to which resistance develops are strongly dependent on the type of bacterial species and type of drug. Models includes natural biofilm development cycle.

Intelligent Drug Agent:

We have simulated multi-drug environments with the intelligent Drug agent. We have simulated the relationships between antibiotic concentrations, bactericidal activity in dynamic environment with deep convolutional neural network. This technique automatically learn the best feature representation from the training data. Interactions between drugs are also modeled. In some cases we find that antibiotic resistance to some synergistic combinations evolves faster than resistance to individual drugs.

Phage Agent

Phage is a type of virus that infects bacteria. Phage will only kill a bacterium if it matches to the specific strain. Bacteria behave differently when they are exposed to phages. Phage-bacteria interactions are unique in that phage interactions with bacteria can range from predatory, to parasitic. Different types of interactions lead to different evolutionary scenarios for the host population, and different genomic signatures. The use of phages against pathogenic bacteria can be modeled using two different approaches, one passive, the other active. Different bacteria–phage interactions occur depending on the health status and development stage of the human host.

Minimal Bacterial Gene Set

A minimal gene set (MGS) is defined as the smallest possible gene set necessary and sufficient to maintain a living organism. Computational analysis has extensively used to try to get closer to the minimal gene set to represent a bacteria. The gene set must contain all the information to allow the cell to perform many essential (housekeeping) functions that give the cell the ability to maintain metabolic homeostasis, reproduce, and evolve, the three main properties of living cells. Researchers have designed and synthesized a minimal bacterial genome, containing only the genes necessary for life, and consisting of just 473 genes. However, the following 38 genes associated with pathogenicity are considered for the initial AI model: crl, ireA, cnf1/2, tia, sat, fyuA, mat, sfa/focCD, malX, afa/drab, neuC, iha, hrlA, fimC, pic, hlyA, kpsMTII, sitDep, ompA, iroN1, gimB, sitD, tratT, ibeA, chuA, vat, tsh, iucD, cvi/cva, papC, irp2, iss, EAST1, felA, iutA, cvaC, papG, fimH.

AI for predicting behaviors of bacteria and phages

Predicting phenotype of bacteria and phages from genotype with deep reinforcement learning algorithms is comparatively easy. The genotype is the set of genes in the DNA which is responsible for a particular trait. The phenotype is the physical expression, or characteristics, of that trait. Genotype is what makes the trait - the information within a gene. Phenotype is what you see - the visible or observable expression of the results of genes. DNA sequencing. The use of artificial intelligence makes finding the right phage much easier, turning the strategy into a more practical treatment option for antibiotic resistance bacteria.

We have discussed here the architecture of the artificial intelligence based system to combat antibiotic resistance bacteria. This is a complex multi-agent master-slave hierarchical deep reinforcement learning system. In this model there are several issues to be resolved. Tuning the models and determining the parameter of the reinforcement learning and CNN of the AI based multi-agent antibiotic resistance bacteria model is a critical issue. However, the initial experimental results show that the proposed approach is promising and effective.

Chapter - 10

Compassionate AI Based Healthcare

Recent advances in AI, especially "Deep Learning" has radically pushed the boundaries of what is possible, enabling a rich set of applications, which were even unthinkable before. AI is widely being used in many aspects of healthcare. AI has enabled the computer algorithms to approximate conclusions without direct human input.

Use of AI in Healthcare

The main areas of AI applications in healthcare are: providing personalized precision medicine, analysis and interpretation of radiology images, automated diagnosis, prescription preparation, clinical workflow monitoring, patient monitoring and care, discovery of new drugs, predicting the impact of gene edits, and development of treatment protocols. Some healthcare systems have even developed digital nurses to help people monitor patient's condition and follow up with treatments, between doctor visits. The programs use machine learning to support patients, specializing in chronic illnesses.

Late detection of disease significantly increases treatment costs and reduces survival rates. Often visual human interpretation of an isolated image is time-consuming, difficult and expensive. With artificial intelligence, it is possible to analyze and interpret large amounts of radiological images efficiently. Recently, AI for radiology uses deep learning, reinforcement learning, and other machine learning algorithms to systematically assess x-ray, CT Scans and MRI images, and instantly provide detailed reports on the findings.

The AI systems are trained using vast numbers of images like CT scans, magnetic resonance imaging (MRI) and ultrasound or nuclear imaging. AI algorithms read medical images like a radiologist. They identify the hidden patterns in the image and relate them with medical data.

Medical institutions such as The Mayo Clinic, Massachusetts General Hospital and National Health

Service have developed AI algorithms for their departments. AI based apps are using AI to give medical consultation based on personal medical history and common medical knowledge. Users report their symptoms into the app, which then uses speech recognition to compare against a database of illnesses, and offers a recommended action, taking into account the user's medical history.

Cardiology and radiology are two medical disciplines where the amount of data to analyze can be overwhelming and time consuming. Analyzing tests, X-Rays, CT scans, and other routine tasks can all be done faster and more accurately by AI agents. In near future, cardiologists and radiologists should only look at the most complicated cases, where human supervision is useful.

AI for the Analysis of Big Data

Healthcare is one of the most data-rich industries, driven by digital health, radiology images, and widespread electronic health records (EHRs) adoption. The smartphone and health tracker revolutions under the name of digital health, available genome sequencing, advanced biotechnology, the health sensors used by the patients at home – have all been producing a vast amount of data. It is increasingly becoming impossible for a physician to analyze all those data and provide the best medicine.

Data from entire patient populations can be efficiently analyzed using AI to discover new evidences and determine best healthcare practices.

AI for Lifestyle Impact Analysis

By observing and analyzing our daily behaviors such as diet, sleep, working style, time management, social interactions and individual's preferences, we may monitor our daily physical, chemical and mental stress. Machine learning algorithms can learn user's behavioral trend and analyze the states of stress.

AI for Genome Sequencing

Machine learning techniques are most useful for linking genotype with phenotype, behavior and environment. Machine leaning technologies can be applied for public personal genome data set to learn the genetic risk for different individuals and groups. AI learning systems can be developed for sophisticated prediction algorithms for incorporating multiple genes and multiple environment factors.

AI Algorithms used in Healthcare

The primary machine learning algorithms used for AI based healthcare systems include linear regression, logistic regression, naive Bayes, decision tree, nearest neighbor, random forest, discriminant analysis, support vector machine (SVM) and neural network. However, among these algorithms, support vector machine (SVM) and neural network are most popular and effective. Currently, deep learning and deep reinforcement algorithms are used for analysis and interpretation of radiological images like CT scan, MRI and nuclear images.

Chapter - 11

Compassionate AI and Precision Medicine

The success of compassionate AI lies in how it can handle the four painful aspects of human life; disease, old age, death and the handicap. As defined by the National Institute of Health (NIH), precision medicine is an emerging approach for disease treatment and prevention that takes into account individual variability in genes, environment, and lifestyle. Big data is a major driver in the development of precision medicine. In other words, precision medicine offers a path to helping people recover from illness faster – and stay healthy longer. AI leverages deep reinforcement learning algorithms to overcome the obstacles inherent in large data sets and also unstructured data. In clinical settings, AI based systems function as an assistant that helps clinicians work more efficiently and make more accurate diagnosis, which in turn helps to improve the productivity of healthcare professionals and provide better experiences for the patients.

Six Dimensions Precision Medicine

Following are the six dimensions of Compassionate AI based precision medicine: evidence, rapid learning & adaptability, gene based precision medicine, identification and detection of drug Interaction, unlimited emotional support and elimination of the risk of over-diagnosis. Over-diagnosis is a widespread malady in the healthcare today that comes from cultural beliefs like "more is better", financial incentives to do more, and expanding disease definitions.

Evidence-based medicine is gradually shifting from therapy to prevention and towards individually tailored precision medicine systems, where, artificial intelligence can be used to automatically detect problems and threats to patient safety, such as patterns of sub-optimal care or outbreaks of hospital-acquired illness. New biomarkers are being identified to predict or detect a wide range of diseases, and new devices are being developed continuously to monitor biological parameters, which are often connected with mobile devices to provide user friendly updates of health status. The optimistic view is that these new diagnostics will transform medicine from treating disease to promoting health, from being reactive to being proactive, and from being general to being personal. There is no doubt that machine learning and advanced AI technologies are enabling a new type of healthcare that focuses on providing individualized precision medicine and emotional support system.

What is Precision Medicine?

Precision medicine is a new scientific way to treat and prevent illnesses tailored to individual on the basis of a person's genes, family history, medical history, evidence, lifestyle, and environment. Precision medicine allows scientists and clinicians to predict more accurately which therapeutic and preventive approaches to a specific illness can work effectively in subgroups of patients based on their genetic make-up, lifestyle, and environmental factors. Precision medicine is also known as molecular based personalized, predictive, preventive and participatory medicine. Precision medicine is powered by patient data, health records and genetic codes of patients.

The precision medicine can implemented only by incorporating many diverse types of data, from genomes to microbiomes, with patient data collected by health care providers and patients themselves through electronics health devices. The main advantage of precision medicine is that it will bring more new therapeutic strategies, drug discovery and development, and gene-oriented treatment for the individual.

Scope of AI in Precision Medicine

With machine learning as the backbone, each person's progress helps the AI systems to improve its platform and make it smarter and more scalable. AI based deep learning systems provides deep interactions with AI coaches and AI therapists, and also enables a range of unlimited live chats to video sessions, depending on the needs of the individual.

Artificial intelligence in healthcare and precision medicine has enormous potential. Machine learning algorithms and other optimization algorithms for large scale data can be applied to find meaningful patterns, insights and knowledge from the combination of genomic data, phenotypic biomarker data, self-reported observational lifestyle data and environmental data. Machine learning algorithms are used for analysis and interpretation of radiology images like CT scans, X-rays and MRIs.

Genome wide association studies (GWAS) are commonly used for detecting associations between single-nucleotide polymorphisms (SNPs) and common diseases such as heart disease, diabetes, auto-immune diseases, and psychiatric disorders. Artificial Intelligence for Genomics sequencing help medical professionals to interpret how genetic variation affects metabolism, DNA repair, and cell growth. Machine learning algorithms are designed based on patterns identified in large genetic data sets.

Artificial intelligence can also be used to prevent the issues over-diagnosis, over-treatment and under-treatment. Artificial intelligence uncovers hidden patterns, unknown correlations, and other insights through examining large-scale varying data sets. Genome sequencing is the dominant platform for using artificial intelligence based precision medicine.

Moreover, the clinical implementation of precision medicine requires reliable data sharing. Blockchain technology can provide that facility to implement precision medicine in practice. The greatest strength of blockchain is a lack of centralized management and ownership. Blockchain uses distributed digital ledger technology. Here patients can participate in managing their own records. No one can tamper the data. Blockchain-based clinical workflow system can assist healthcare organizations in monitoring the entire life cycle of the treatments and transactions.

Currently, evidence-based medicine is unable to solve the issues like hospital-acquired illness, drug-interaction and antibiotic resistant bacteria. Artificial intelligence with precision medicine can be used for solving issues like hospital-acquired illness, drug-interaction and antibiotic resistant bacteria by developing individual genetics and large scale population based modeling.

Convolution neural network based Multifactor Dimensionality Reduction (MDR) feature construction methods are often used for modeling higher-order feature interactions. It can be combined with expert knowledge-guided feature selector for large biomedical data sets.

AI to Prevent Drug Interaction

Drug interactions, including drug-drug interactions (DDIs) and drug-food constituent interactions (DFIs), can trigger unexpected pharmacological effects on patients, including adverse drug events (ADEs). It has been shown that drug-drug interactions (DDI) are a significant cause of hospital admissions in the elderly population. Improved DDI information could help reduce such adverse effects. Still, physicians and health professionals admit a lack of data and tools that meet their needs and are clinically relevant. A large problem in this area is the management of drug-related information and data. With the help of AI, a deep learning platform can be used to develop clinically relevant tools for pharmacists and physicians for efficiently predicting how drugs might adversely interact with other drugs or food.

Compassionate AI for Emotional Support to Patients

Machine learning and advanced AI technologies are enabling a new type of care that focuses on providing individualized emotional support. Compassionate AI systems have huge potential in healthcare and caregiving for patients suffering from mental problems, depression and other such diseases. While human caregivers are prone to face the risk of burn-outs in the long run, compassionate AI systems can provide endless emotional support for patients who need them.

AI agents can recognize not only words but also nonverbal cues, for example, facial expression, gestures or posture. Nonverbal signs are very important in therapy, yet can be subtle and difficult to pick up. The ability to constantly sense the emotions of the patients will enable the AI agents to acquire an emotion profile of the patients over a period of time as well as record their responses to specific regulating strategies used. Over time this emotion profile shall become a knowledge base for each patient. Such knowledge base would enable the AI agents to identify effective regulating strategies that are unique to each patient under a certain treatment regime.

There is another advantage of an AI agent over a human therapist. Normally people find it easier to share potentially embarrassing information with an AI based bot. In human-to-human interaction, there is often a degree of self-restraint or shame, which can prevent people from sharing openly with another person. However, when communicating with an AI bot, patients are reported to feel more at ease, and they may share their information more frankly, which could have an important therapeutic advantage. In addition, AI bots are always available and can offer therapeutic interactions more often compared to a human therapist.

Compassionate AI to Remove Social Isolation

We are entering a very interesting period for humanity. With advancement in AI, much of our day to day problems will be solved by AI agents. Extreme social isolation and difficulties in building close relationships are often a cause of depression among the youths. The problem of social isolation and loneliness that are increasing day by day can be solved with the help of compassionate AI chat-bots and other AI agents designed to serve this end.

Social networks on the Internet often foster a sense of belonging and encourage positive communication. AI agents can be designed to provide emotional support to lonely elders or young people, to make them feel loved, secure and to elevate their moods. With the advances in natural language processing AI driven chat-bots are used to provide such help. They are constantly improving to become more human-like and natural.

Cellular-Reprogramming for Compassionate AI

Cellular reprogramming, nuclear reprogramming, direct neuronal reprogramming, epigenetic editing and genome editing technologies has opened up unprecedented opportunities for health, well-being and higher human consciousness with intelligence and compassion. Reprogramming is the process of changing one cell type into a different cell type and creating new cell types.

John Gurdon and Shinya Yamanaka, received the 2012 Nobel Prize for Physiology or Medicine for their groundbreaking work on "the discovery that mature cells can be reprogrammed to become pluripotent." They discovered ways to take an ordinary cell, such as a skin cell, and "reprogram" it by introducing several genes that convert it into a pluripotent cell. These genetically reprogrammed cells are known as induced pluripotent cells, or iPS cells. Pluripotent means capable of giving rise to several different cell types. Pluripotent cells are master cells. They're able to make cells from the three basic body layers of the cell, so they can potentially produce any cell or tissue the body needs to repair itself. This "master" property is called pluripotency. Like all stem cells, pluripotent cells are also able to self-renew, meaning they can perpetually create more copies of themselves.

Cloning in mammals invited strong reactions in the society, as it raised the vision of unethical human cloning, which could be misused. To stop growing public concerns, a nonbinding United Nations Declaration called for the ban of all forms of human cloning in 2005. However, the research on human induced pluripotent stem cells (hiPSCs) does not suffer from the same ethical constraints as research on human embryonic stem cells (ESCs), which requires precious human embryos.

AI provides a new tool to study the mechanisms of reprogramming that may lead to more improvements in iPS cell production and safety. AI can be effectively used to eventually develop powerful iPS cell therapeutics. Artificial intelligence based agents can be trained to examine genetic changes that occur in individual cells as they become pluripotent.

Apart from cellular reprogramming, AI based algorithms can also be used for direct neuronal reprogramming. AI agents can also be used for epigenetic editing, by resetting the time clock. The machine learning algorithms can be used to find out the best strategy to avoid any genetic manipulation and overexpression of enhancing genes.

Big data sets of human genomes and their corresponding phenotypes — the physical and mental characteristics of the individual, will lead to significant progress in our ability to understand the genetic code and in particular, to enhance human cognitive ability. Studies suggest that millions of phenotype-genotype pairs will be required to edit and predict the genetic architecture. Advanced AI based machine learning algorithms can be used for this purpose.

Millions of patterns of human cognitive behavior is hidden within millions of phenotype-genotype pairs. AI systems like convolutional neural networks based deep learning can be used to identify and predict the hidden patterns. AI systems can act with high precision for cell reprogramming, epigenetic editing and genome based prediction of intelligence. AI systems can help in developing predictive models that can be used in active genetic editing. With the advancement of these technologies, super-intelligent and super-compassionate humans can be a reality which will coevolve and jointly participate with compassionate and super-intelligent AI systems, forming the basis of distributed human-machine intelligence network of Compassionate AI.

Chapter - 12

Artificial Intelligence with Emotional Intelligence

Modern AI has been tremendously successful for pattern recognition, voice recognition, face identification and machine learning. Self-driven cars are already on road in testing phase. But, in today's world AI is more needed in dealing with removal of human suffering on the mental and emotional levels.

Modern technological advances is increasingly applied to systems where they can interact with humans emotionally and intelligently. The most widely addressed area of research in automated emotion recognition is the recognition of facial expressions. Physiological information has been shown to carry information that changes with different emotions.

Handling of emotions, in others as well as in oneself, requires emotional intelligence. Integration of AI with emotional intelligence are expected to work in favor of humans.

Compassionate AI is needed to deal with emotions like anger, impatience, disappointment, frustration, and turning them in to peace, patience, awe, surprise, hope, joy and gratitude. In the following pages, we'll cover the scope, issues and challenges of AI for developing emotional intelligence in machines.

Currently, deep learning modules of AI based systems lack the emotional aspects of human intelligence. However, AI is expanding and evolving itself in many technological fronts. It is not only limited by Deep learning algorithms, but expanding its horizons in deeper levels of human consciousness.

To fix the emotional and subjective issues like relationship, depression, anxiety and such other emotional issues, future artificial intelligence based systems like cyborgs require deep emotional intelligence modules. A cyborg (short for "cybernetic organism") is a being with both organic and bio-mechanical-electronic body parts. A cyborg in AI systems can be a bio-mechatronic bridge between the inner world and the outer world — a bridge between mind, matter and consciousness.

A compassionate cyborg is that which tries to minimize human sufferings like anxiety, depression, hatred, jealousy, anger, fear and frustration. Development of a compassionate AI cyborg will lead to a jump in the quality of human consciousness.

Need for Combining AI with Emotional Intelligence

Emotions are essential part of human intelligence. Without emotional intelligence, AI is incomplete. Human emotion is deeply associated with motivation, decision, evaluation, learning, character, intelligence, desires, and awareness. Nearly all human psychological activities are subject to emotional influences and excitation. Self-awareness is one of the most significant mental faculties of a human being. It gives us the capacity to assess our emotional states. Hence, self-awareness is one of vital elements of human intelligence. Therefore, if we are to take the development of artificial intelligence to the next level, we should take account of the core ideas like self-awareness and emotional intelligence.

Emotional intelligence is defined as the ability to recognize, understand and manage one's own emotions and to recognize and influence the emotions of others. Obviously, emotional intelligence separates us from the machines. It includes the ability to identify emotions, to recognize their powerful effects, and to use that information to guide our behavior. Emotional intelligence includes the ability to influence and evoke strong emotions in others, with a view to persuading or motivating them.

Strategies for Integrating AI with EI

Presently, AI is being increasingly dependent on cloud computing, IoT and big data. Our goal is to model the range of higher human emotions, as well as their inner dynamics.

There are different frameworks, libraries, applications, toolkits, and datasets in the AI and machine learning world. By creating a direct neural interface with the

Internet libraries, applications and frameworks, humankind will be able to "plug into" higher intelligence.

The five components of AI with emotional intelligence are as follows; deep learning, self-awareness, external awareness, safety and ethics, and big data collection and processing modules. Developing self-awareness of the machine is the first challenge of true AI based systems.

Figure - 11: AI with EI modules

Integrating AI with EI: Issues and Challenges

For integrating advanced artificial intelligence with emotional intelligence, several potential barriers are to be addressed:

Privacy: Many people feel that their emotions are private, and concerns about violations of privacy is genuine. Protective legislation needs to expand to address risks associated with AI, specifically with the collection, storage, transfer and use of confidential emotional data and health information.

Accuracy: AI accuracy in correctly determining emotional intent needs to be confirmed, specifically in regards to system biases or errors, before labeling a person as high or low emotional. False alarms can create danger for the person involved.

Safety: It is essential to ensure that AI programs can appropriately respond to human users, so as to not worsen their emotional state, or accidentally stimulate adverse response and create hostile situation.

Responsibility: Response protocols are needed to properly handle high risk cases that are identified by compassionate AI technology. There should be clear guidance about what to do, if AI risk assessments differ from human expert's opinion.

Lack of understanding: There is likely to be a knowledge gap among experts and key users on how AI technology fits into emotional understanding of humans. More education on the topic is needed to address this issue.

Chapter - 13

Quantum Computing and Compassionate AI

In the following pages, we will discusses the power, scope, and challenges of Quantum Computing and Artificial Intelligence in details. These two technologies are evolving and growing at an exponential rate to reach a state, where each will deeply influence the other.

In recent years there has been an explosion of interest in quantum computing and artificial intelligence — the two parallel fields. Quantum computing with artificial intelligence could revolutionize our society and bring many benefits. Big companies like IBM, Google, Microsoft and Intel are all currently racing to build useful quantum computer systems. They have also made tremendous progress in developing deep learning and machine intelligence systems.

Artificial intelligence (AI) is an area of science that emphasizes the development of intelligent systems, which can work and behave like humans. Quantum computing is essentially using the amazing laws of quantum mechanics to enhance computing power. These two emergent technologies will likely have huge transforming impact on our society in the future. Quantum computing is becoming a vital platform to provide speed-ups for machine learning problems, critical to big data analysis, blockchain and IoT.

There are two main reasons to discuss quantum computing and artificial intelligence in this section. First is introducing the basic ideas of quantum computers, and the second purpose is how they can be used to implement the full power of artificial intelligence in solving real world problems. Especially, quantum neural networks is the next natural step in the evolution of quantum-neuro-computing systems.

Quantum computing deals with developing computing power using the laws of quantum mechanics of particle physics. Classical physics applies to things we can see, touch and feel with our five senses, whereas quantum physics applies to the world at the scale of atoms and subatomic levels. Quantum particles can move forward or backward in time, exist in two states, simultaneously, and even “teleport” irrespective of distances.

Just as a traditional digital computer requires that the data be encoded into binary digits (bits), each of which is always in one of two definite states 0 or 1, a quantum bits (qubits) is the basic unit of information in a quantum computer. Unlike classical computing, where each bit represents either a 0 or a 1, but not both at once, a quantum bit can simultaneously superpose 0 and 1 and only resolves (or "collapses") to a single value when measured.

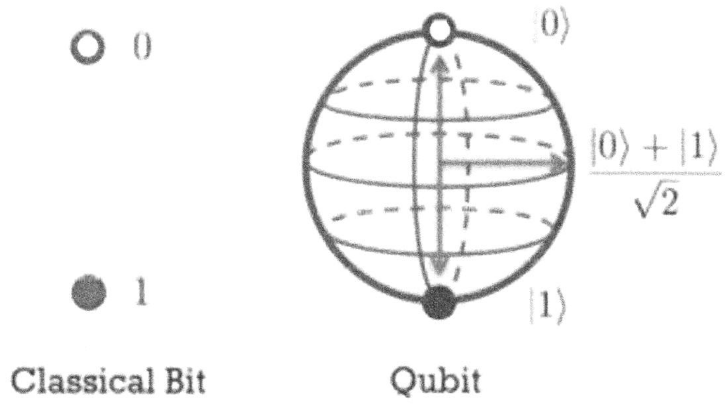

Figure – 12: Quantum bit or qubit

A quantum bit (qubit) can be thought of like an imaginary sphere, whereas a traditional bit can be in two states – at either of the two poles of the sphere. A quantum bit can be any point on the sphere. This means a computer using these bits can store a huge amount of information using less energy and space than a classical computer. So rather than having bits that can only be 1 or 0 at any given moment, qubits can be anything and everything at once. This means they can perform many calculations simultaneously, giving them the potential for unparalleled processing power. So, while a bit represents just 1 or 0, one qubit represents an array of possibilities, and all can be calculated simultaneously taking probabilities in account.

Qubits represent the sates of atoms, ions, photons or electrons and their respective control devices that work together to act as computer memory and a processor. While a classical computer operates serially, essentially dealing with one bit after another, a quantum computer's qubits interact parallel. Because a quantum computer can contain these multiple states simultaneously, it has the potential to be millions of times more powerful than today's most powerful traditional supercomputers.

Power of Quantum Computing

Quantum computing uses mainly two properties of quantum particles followed by the laws of quantum mechanics: the principles of superposition of states and the concept of entanglement. Superposition is a "one-particle" property, while entanglement is the characteristic of two or more particles.

The ability to process the zeros and ones at the same time gives tremendous power. Thus a relatively small quantum computer could surpass the most powerful classical supercomputers.

The power of quantum computing is limited by the number of qubits. Quantum entanglement enables the quantum computers to principally perform many calculations at once. And the number of such calculations should, in principle, double for each additional qubit, leading to an exponential speed-up.

Quantum computers can solve problems that are impossible or would take a traditional computer an unrealistic amount of time (a billion years) to solve. Once the development of quantum computer gets settled, the time for machine learning will exponentially speed up, even reducing the time to solve a problem from hundreds of thousands of years to seconds.

A quantum computer containing of 500 qubits would have a potential to do 2^{500} calculations in a single step. This is an awesome number. The number 2^{500} signifies infinitely more atoms than there are in our known universe.

A 30 qubits quantum computer will have computing power equivalent to 10 teraflops classical computer. To exceed the limits of classical computing, computers of at least 50 to 100 qubits are needed. Advances in quantum communication and quantum cryptography, which rely heavily on extending entanglement, could change the way information is stored, processed and transferred in the future.

Artificial Intelligence and Quantum Computing

Artificial intelligence has five generations, as discussed earlier. Quantum computing can be used in all the five generations of AI. However, they are especially needed in the higher order AI systems. Especially, quantum computing and quantum neural networks learning algorithms have promises to design compassion and emotional intelligence parts in higher AI based systems.

Quantum Neural Networks

Integrating quantum computing with training and implementation of artificial neural networks has been studied by many researches (Liu, Chen, Chang, & Shih, 2013). Presently, deep learning algorithms have achieved "superhuman" levels of perception. New quantum algorithms of machine learning based on qubits like Quantum Convolutional Neural Nets (QCNN) and Quantum Reinforcement Neural Network (QRNN) or (QRL) (Fösel, Tighineanu, Weiss, & Marquardt, 2018) are rapidly developing a new era of AI. In reinforcement learning (RL), control strategies are improved according to a reward function. A reinforcement learning agent interacts with its environment in discrete time steps. Researchers observed that quantum neural networks can be trained efficiently using gradient descent on a cost function to perform quantum generalizations of classical tasks (Wan, Dahlsten, Kristjánsson, Gardner, & Kim, 2016).

Current State of quantum Computing

We are on the verge of a new age of human discovery with quantum computing. A full-fledged true quantum computer is yet to be invented, and still appears years away, but quantum computing operations can be carried out on today's qubit hardware. IBM has developed a number of quantum computer systems ranging from 5 to 50 qubits. Currently, big companies like IBM, Google, Intel, and Microsoft are positioning themselves as first movers in establishing the era of commercial quantum computing. Quantum computing will give power to the AI for developing higher levels super-intelligent systems.

Limitations of Quantum Computing

Quantum information is extremely fragile and it requires special techniques to preserve the quantum state. The qubits are extremely sensitive to environmental noise. This can be noise from outside the device like temperature, radiations, vibration etc. Noises can also come from inside like in the cooling system, microwave cabling, and the chip components themselves. Generally, the quantum systems requires special infrastructures to produce ultra-cold liquid helium of about -460 degrees Fahrenheit. This difficulty of developing and maintaining a cold enough environment for a quantum computer to operate is the main reason they are still at the experimental stage, and now can only process a few qubits at a time.

Chapter - 14

Internet of Things (IoT) and Compassionate AI

Internet is a powerful tool used in all kinds of information systems. The internet network is available almost anywhere, at home, at car, at work, also on mobile devices. People started to connect the Internet to almost all devices of everyday use, so they can communicate with each other and help them in their daily lives. Such idea is called the Internet of Things (IoT) (Poniszewska-Maranda & Kaczmarek, 2015). Modern trend of Internet is commonly referred to as Internet-of-Everything, which includes Internet-of-Things (IoT), Internet-of-Medical-Things (IoMT), Internet-of-Battlefield-Things (IoBT), Internet-of-Vehicles (IoV), and so on.

The scope of IoT is unlimited, and may include devices such as heart monitoring implants, biochip transponders, automobile sensors, aerospace and defense field operation devices, and public safety applications that assist fire-fighters etc. It also includes smart phones, home appliances, toys, cameras, medical instruments, vehicles and industrial systems.

It can also include animals and people, when chips are attached in the body parts, internally or externally. IoT enriches mass data collection, automation, operation, and much more, through smart devices and powerful enabling technology. Gartner has estimated that by 2016 there will be 6.4 billion connected devices in use, and this number is further expected to hit 20.8 billion by 2020.

7 Characteristics of Internet of Things

The seven main characteristics of IoT are as follows:

1. **Connectivity:** IoT refers to the connection of all types of heterogeneous devices. It also includes connection of diverse communications networks, protocols and embedded technologies.
2. **Things:** "Things", in the IOT sense, can refer to a wide variety of devices, which include household appliances, commodity sensors, and embedded systems.
3. **Networks:** Heterogeneous networks can co-exist on a much simple and complex systems.

Anything that can be tagged or connected to such networks, from sensors and household appliances to tagged livestock, falls under it.

4. **Data:** Data is the heart of the Internet of Things. The exponential growth of big data perfectly matches with that of IoT. The amount of devices that connect to the internet will rise from about 13 billion today to 28 billion by 2020 (Nordrum, 2016). IoT dramatically increases the amount of data available for us to process. The more data is created, the more information, knowledge and wisdom can be obtained. Big data is commonly follow the principles of five "V's" - Volume, Visibility, Velocity, Variety, and Value.

5. **Interoperability:** Interoperability is a key challenge in the domains of the Internet of Things (IoT). Interoperability is the ability of diverse information technology systems and software applications to communicate, exchange data, and use the information that has been exchanged.

   In IoT, future networks will continue to be heterogeneous, multi-vendors, multi-services and largely distributed. IoT must adhere to four types of interoperability. They are technical interoperability, Syntactical Interoperability,

Semantic Interoperability, and Organizational Interoperability (Patel & Patel, 2016).

6. **The Spectrum of Insight:** IOT must have the ability to get insight from the big data. Data analytics will be executed at five main computing levels – sensor level, network level, cloud level, server level, and client level. Hence insight from the big data in the IoT can be extracted across various locations and time.
7. **Safety, Security and Privacy:** Privacy of data by design is becoming the key issue of IoT. This includes the privacy of personal data, security of military data, and the safety and physical well-being of humans. Securing the endpoints, the networks, and the data processing is vital. AI based security models are must for implementing safety, security and privacy needs.

Compassionate AI with IoT:

Compassionate AI agents will work in the following five levels in an integrated fashion: – sensor level, network level, cloud level, server level, and client level. AI can be used with IoT in the following four main areas:

1) Intelligent sensors, 2) Intelligent communication networks, 3) big-data analysis with machine learning, and 4) AI based monitoring and controlling.

In healthcare services, IoT allows patients to receive care at home where they're most comfortable. Medical devices are becoming increasingly intelligent, connected, and robust for delivering optimized healthcare services. With wearable sensors, doctors can remotely track and respond to a patient's health status in real time.

In healthcare, IoT and AI based activity trackers will assist in logging activity, and allow doctors to keep accurate and track of whether patients are sticking to their treatment plan and allow them to make changes, where necessary. IoT and compassionate AI based activity trackers will also remind the patients of their drug timings and necessary changes in lifestyle in a caring and friendly manner. For example, it can track antipsychotic and hypertension pill adherence, remind a patient for a medical check-up, and also provide early advices for prevention.

Compassionate AI with IoT are opening up new doors to conduct clinical trials, so that testing a potential new drug would integrate lifestyle data, which can simulate the effect of a new drug for a patient with a particular lifestyle. CAI with IoT can also be used to forecast how a new therapy is going to affect a particular patient already on a drug.

Compassionate AI can be used for discovering patterns from connected health monitoring devices, radiology images, lab reports as well as patient history, providing tremendous opportunities for preventive care.

In many other areas like home appliances and customer services, compassionate AI and IoT can be used for interacting with people with courteous and polite attitude.

Chapter - 15

Brain-Computer interface and Compassionate AI

Brain Computer Interface (BCI) is a rapidly emerging multidisciplinary research field. A brain-computer interface (BCI) is a technology that allows communication between a human or animal brain and an external technology. A brain–computer interface can translate neuronal information into commands capable of controlling external software or hardware such as a computer or robotic arm, or a keyboard. A brain-computer interface may also be known as a brain-machine interface (BMI), a direct neural interface, or a mind-machine interface.

The central theory of BMI is the capacity to distinguish different patterns of brain activity, each being associated to a particular intention or mental task (Del R. Millán & Carmena, 2010).

In essence, BCI or BMI establishes two way communications between the brain and the machine.

BMIs are often used as assisted living devices for individuals with motor or sensory impairments. Thus, BCI hopes to create new communication channels for disabled or elderly persons using their brain signals.

BCI extracts specific features from the brain signals that reflect the intent of the subject, and translates these features into actions that controls an object (such as moving a wheelchair or selecting a letter from a virtual keyboard), without using the activity of any muscle or peripheral nerve. BMI represents a promising technology for paralyzed patients, as it does not need muscle engagement for its use.

Brain Signals

The human brain contains, on average, about 86 billion nerve cells called neurons, each individually linked to other neurons by way of connectors called axons and dendrites. Signals at the junctures (synapses) of these connections are transmitted by the release and detection of chemicals known as neurotransmitters. Every time we think, feel, move, or remember something, our neurons are at work.

The brain generates enormous amount of neural activities. The neuronal activities are carried out by small electric signals or impulses that travels from neuron to neuron at very high speed, as fast as 250 mph. Our “mind” is a thinking machine generating thoughts and emotions by a set of processes carried out by the neurons of the brain.

The electric signals that travels from neuron to neuron are generated by differences in electric potential carried by ions on the membrane of each neuron. There are a plethora of signals, which can be used for BCI. These signals are divided into two classes: spikes and field potentials. Although the paths the signals take are insulated by a sheath called myelin, some of the electric signal escapes. In BCI, scientists can detect those signals, interpret what they mean, and use them to direct a device of some kind.

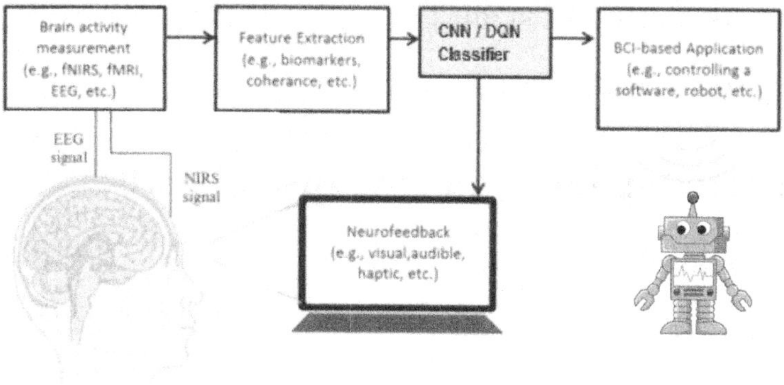

Figure – 13: Brain computer interface arrangements

Types of Brain Computer Interface (BCI)

Brain computer interface can be classified into three main groups: Non-Invasive, Semi-invasive and Invasive. In invasive BCI techniques, special devices need to be used to capture the brain signals. Invasive BCI devices are inserted directly into the human brain by a critical surgery. Invasive methods in humans remain severely limited in their practical usefulness.

In Semi-invasive BCI, devices are inserted in the skull on the top of human brain. Non-Invasive BCI devices are considered the safest and low cost type of devices. However, the human brain signals captured these devices are weaker than other BCI devices due to the obstruction of the skull. The detection of signals is done by some electrodes placed on the scalp.

Brain Signal Acquiring Instruments:

Functional magnetic resonance imaging (fMRI), positron emission tomography (PET), magneto-encephalography (MEG), and scalp electroencephalography (EEG), are commonly used for non-invasive BCI study. However, the research data collected by these devices are characterized by bulkiness, high cost, high sensitivity to head movements, low spatial and temporal resolution, and low signal quality.

Near Infrared Spectroscopy (NIRS) is a novel optical imaging modality, for noninvasive, continuous monitoring of tissue oxygenation, and regional blood flow in brain. NIRS is not only non-invasive and safe, but also portable, affordable, and requires short setup time, which makes it more user-friendly. Wireless NIRS systems are also available, which enable the monitoring of brain activity in moving subjects, such as walking or running people.

The use of Functional NIRS (fNIRS) is relatively new, which uses near-infrared-range light (usually of 650 ~ 1000 nm wavelength) to measure the concentration changes of oxygenated hemoglobin (HbO) and deoxygenated hemoglobin (HbR). Compared to fMRI, fNIRS offers lower spatial resolution and provides higher temporal resolution.

Advances in BCI Research

The earliest brain-computer interface technologies simply recorded signals from the brain. More modern BCI technologies are designed as implants that will improve on skills associated with certain brain activities, such as vision, hearing, or other human or animal functions. A range of these devices, called neuroprosthetics, have been developed and are in use around the world as a functional means of assisting human capabilities.

Over the last 5 years, technologies for non-invasive transmission of information from brains to computers have developed considerably. This research is going to be immensely beneficial for the physically and mentally challenged people as well as for the people who are suffering from post-traumatic stress disorder (PTSD), and other mental disorders or neurological problems.

Researchers focus to build a direct communication link between the human brain and the smartphones, earphone, computers or other devices. With BCI, mind can speak silently with a smartphone or other devices. Recent advancement of neuroprosthetic, linking the human nervous system to computers, providing unprecedented control of artificial limbs and restoring lost sensory function has shown much promise for the use of this technology for the physically or mentally challenged.

Link between Compassionate AI and BCI

BCI research also created hopes to remove fearful thoughts, disturbing thoughts, feelings and bad dreams of any common people. Artificial intelligence can be another modern type of brain-computer interface that can be used for multiple purposes.

With the advancement and exploration of new mobile bio-monitoring devices, earphones, neuroprosthetic, wireless wearable intelligent sensors, it is becoming possible to monitor the activities of the neurons in the human brain. The small intelligent sensors can notice the brain activities, and synchronize them with the mobile devices. The noninvasive devices are also used to measure the brain activities, people's emotions, their interactions with others, and their bio-metric changes under different conditions.

The role of compassionate AI is to help the sick and physically and mentally challenged people who are suffering a lot. With BCI the intelligent sensors will capture the brain signals and compassionate AI will interpret that and take suitable kind action to eliminate the pain.

AI based BCI has tremendous scope to remove the suffering of the humanity. BCI based on AI can send signals to the brain combining the rapport-building skills of human caregiver with the feelings of love, care, protection, forgiveness and safety. By sending signals of a welcoming expression and posture, and being attentive, loving and responsive, AI-based BCI can help many patients and people who are suffering from mental disorders.

The purpose of Compassionate AI is to remove the pain from the society and help humanity. Artificial Intelligence with Brain-Computer Interface (BCI) or Brain Machine Interface (BMI) can be very effective to achieve this end.

However, the integration of these emerging technologies and brain computer interfaces raise many ethical concerns. Particularly, the research work for mind upload or brain upload (often called as "mind copying" or "mind transfer") has privacy, safety and ethical concerns involved.

Convolution Neural Network and BCI

Convolution Neural Networks (CNN) is a type of artificial neural network inspired by the working of visual cortex of human brain. It has capacity of learning the appropriate features from the input data automatically, by optimizing the weight parameters using filters through the forward and backward propagation in order to minimize the classification error.

Human auditory cortex is arranged in a hierarchical organization, much like the visual cortex. In a hierarchical system, a series of brain regions performs different types of computation on sensory information as it flows through the system. It has been well documented that the visual cortex has this type of organization. Earlier regions, known as the primary visual cortex, respond to simple features such as color or orientation. Later stages enable more complex tasks such as object recognition.

One advantage of using deep learning technique is that it requires minimal pre-processing because optimal settings are learned automatically. One major advantage of CNNs is that feature extraction and classification are integrated into a single structure and optimized automatically. Functional NIRS (fNIRS) time series data of human subjects are used as inputs to the CNN. As the convolution is performed in the sliding window manner, the feature extraction process of CNN retains the temporal information of the time series data obtained by fNIRS. Typical structure of a CNN is given below.

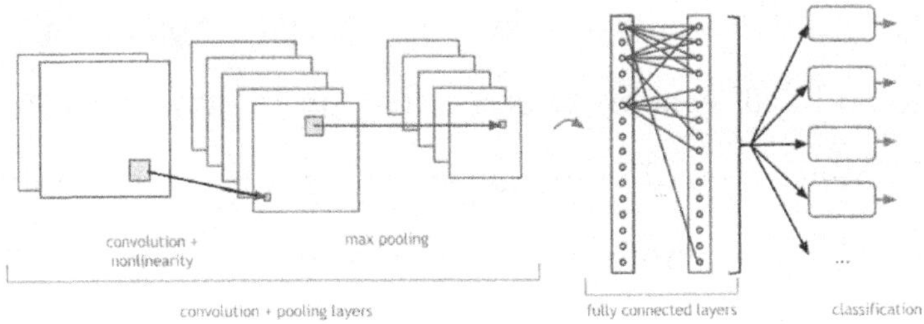

Figure – 14: Convolutional neural network layers

In CNN, after a convolution layer, it is common to add a pooling layer in between CNN layers. The most frequent type of pooling is max pooling, which takes the maximum value in each window.

Reinforcement Learning and BCI

Reinforcement learning is a framework to learn directly from the interaction of agents and environment and thereby achieve desired goals. Agent is defined as an entity that has cognitive skills, the ability to solve the problem, and the ability to communicate with the outside environment.

In reinforcement learning framework, agent is a learner and decision-maker, interacting with environment, which is outside of the agent. Agents choose an action, and the environment responds to the action with reward or punishment. The ultimate goal of agent is to maximize the sum of the rewards in the long term.

There are various frameworks and algorithms for reinforcement learning. Reinforcement learning framework for BCI can use either table-based algorithms (Q-learning, SARSA, SARSA-λ) or neural network-based algorithms (Q-NN, NFQ, DQN, DDQN). The advantage of using neural networks over table-based methods is that the former regulates reinforcement learning with superior generalization and convergence in real-world applications.

The very aim of BCI is to translate brain activity into a command for a computer. One of the biggest problems in BCI research is the non-stationarity of brain signals. Non-stationarity makes it difficult for a classifier to find reliable patterns in the signals, resulting in bad classifying performances. In combination with the RL agent and CNN or other feedback approaches this could improve learning performance to control a BCI and reduce training time.

BCI technology with machine learning algorithms is improving very fast. They are giving ways and means to record and distinguish the signals of the brain neurons. BCI with compassionate AI can provide disabled people with compassionate communication, environment control, and movement restoration. It can allow paralyzed people to control prosthetic limbs with their mind. It can transmit auditory data to the mind of a deaf person, allowing them to hear. It has tremendous scope in many non-medical applications as well, like compassionate caregiving, and brain to brain communication for improving relationships.

Chapter - 16

Drones and Compassionate AI

Literally the word drone means "a continuous low humming sound". However, in a scientific context, drone is an unmanned aircraft. Basically, a drone is a flying robot. It is also known as unmanned aerial vehicle (UAV). These aircrafts may be remotely controlled or can fly autonomously through software-controlled flight plans in their embedded systems working in combination with onboard sensors and GPS.

Uses of Drone

Currently, drones are mainly used for policing, peacekeeping and military surveillance. Main advantages of drones compared to manned systems are that UAVs can fly in inaccessible areas, such as mountainous, volcanic, earthquake, storm tracking and desert areas, flood plains, sights of accidents and the dangerous areas inhabited by the terrorists. Drones are less expensive and have lower operating costs than manned aircrafts. Drones are required to comply with existing flying regulations.

Defense organizations have their own standards, and civilian bodies have their ever-evolving categories for UAV. Normally, drones are classified according to their size, range and endurance, intelligence, combat capability, fixed or rotary wings, and use of tier systems. Typically drones carry video cameras, thermal or infrared camera systems, multispectral cameras, range camera sensors and LiDAR sensors (Eisenbeiss, 2011).

AI and Drones for Emergency Services

The role of compassionate AI based drones is to help the emergency services to keep people safer. The key benefit to using drone technology is in collection of data and the uses of intelligence for prompt decision making. Compassionate AI drones can do the rescue operations quicker, saving time, money, and potentially lives by enabling the debris from an accident to be cleared away more quickly.

Presently, drones are used for surveillance of big events like Olympics to avoid terrorism risks. Drones are also used by police departments for finding missing boats or people in coastal area.

Incorporating Compassionate AI in Drone

Presently AI is used in drone to train the computer vision systems. Skydio's R1 is one such example of use of AI in drone (Statt, 2018). AI algorithms like deep reinforcement learning are used to train to recognize humans, animals and other distinct objects like mountains, rivers, roads, trees and cars. Image recognition, object detection and tracking, computational photography, augmented reality, 3D reconstruction are the main uses of AI in drone systems.

Visual insight is fundamental for all intelligent systems to work. Deep Learning based approach significantly improve their recognition system that was based on traditional computer vision techniques. Under low lighting or arbitrary lighting conditions, drones developed with AI based algorithms work very efficiently.

Compassionate AI based Intelligent Honeybee Drones can be used to counter autonomous weapons. Compassionate AI based Honey-bee Drones can also be used to resist mass destruction by making such weapons defunct.

Chapter – 17

Blockchain and Distributed Compassionate AI

Blockchain is an open distributed ledger that can record transactions between two parties efficiently and in a verifiable and permanent way.

In blockchain technology, there is no central authority to control and manipulate. Hence there would be fewer errors and frauds. Blockchain is a peer-to-peer distributed ledger technology and has three major components:

1. Distributed network: The decentralized peer-to-peer architecture has nodes consisting of network participants, where each member stores an identical copy of the blockchain and is authorized to validate and certify digital transactions for the network.

2. Shared ledger: The members in the network record the ongoing digital transactions into a shared ledger. They run algorithms and verify the proposed transaction, and once a majority of members validate the transaction, it is added to the shared ledger.

3. Digital transaction: Any information or digital asset that could be stored in a blockchain could qualify as a digital block by block transaction. Each transaction is structured into a 'block,' and each block contains a cryptographic hash to add the transactions in a linear, chronological order.

Blockchain disrupted the financial world with cryptocurrencies like Bitcoin and Litecoin. Blockchain uses decentralized technology which has reversed the use of traditional centralized technology. Due to the decentralized technology of database architecture, the record and authentication of operations are performed based on agreement of several other parties rather than a sole authority. One of the main benefits of blockchain technology is that it can be used in many applications beyond cryptocurrency and financial assets.

Blockchain and AI

Artificial intelligence and blockchain have numerous common characteristics which can be seamlessly integrated together to get the benefits of both the technologies. Distributed artificial intelligence is one of the main application areas of blockchain.

Distributed ledger technologies have the potential to help in many areas of AI, especially in the areas of healthcare, communication, transportation, and government applications. The following are some of the areas which help to have a perfect interaction of both artificial intelligence and blockchain.

Decentralized Artificial Intelligence:

Traditional AI follows one agent control centralized system where we get access to the API that is part of a cloud based service. However, in distributed ledger technology the database and the intelligent inference engine can be shared across a network of multiple sites, geographies or institutions. All participants within the network can have their own identical copy of the ledger and the inference engine. The AI agents will be available in a distributed fashion.

Decentralization of AI Data

Presently, the lack of large, publicly available datasets makes adopting AI difficult. Decentralization of training dataset will help to build a collaborative approach to train the data. Blockchain goals to tackle that single issue by introducing the concept of peer-to-peer connection. By keeping all training data on the device, there is no dependence on storing the data in the cloud. Since it is an open distributed registry, the data will be accessible to everyone on the network. Decentralized AI platforms will also promote transparency and give everyone the chance to be an active member of one of the most impactful technologies of our time.

Chapter - 18

Compassionate AI for Next Generation

Serving humanity intelligently is held up as the "gold standard" of AI based systems. Stopping terrorism and nuclear war is also crucial for human survival. The power of AI and nuclear technology should not be misused. Compassion, kindness and empathy are the components of higher human intelligence and to be truly intelligent, artificial intelligence must incorporate them in the system. Rapid progress is being made today in the field of artificial intelligence. These advances will possibly transform every area of the society.

The objective of this book is to motivate researchers and formulate the strategies and framework for the beneficial and compassionate use of the artificial intelligence technology. Right now we are taking baby steps to build and evolve compassionate AI systems. But soon humans will evolve machines that can execute more complex tasks and have much better general intelligence. Ultimately we hope to create truly compassionate superintelligence.

We explained how the emerging technologies like Internet of things (IoT), drones, genetics and cell reprogramming, brain-computer-interface, blockchain and big data can be used with deep learning and other modern artificial intelligence (AI) architectures for the ultimate level of joint evolution of human and machine intelligence.

Here we are not trying to solve all issues and problems of developing compassionate AI. Our work here was an exercise in figuring out the best frameworks and algorithms for implementing an integrated compassionate AI system that can jointly work with humans for creating a better society.

As we have said earlier, compassionate AI is neither a servant, nor a toy that can be manipulated by individual will. CAI will be a distributed, decentralized, and democratized Intelligence that can access the collective intelligence and may have brain to brain communication skill.

Democratization of AI and Security Issues

A large factor that contributed to the explosion of AI in the recent years is the explosion of data. According to Forbes, the amount of data created from 2013 to 2015 is greater than the amount of data created in all of human history before that. Most of these data are created on social media platforms such as Facebook, search engines, such as Google and online or mobile applications.

With these collected data, big companies are able to create extremely sophisticated AI algorithms that help them to create target advertisements to precise audiences, and also manipulate public behavior and decisions. While large data are required to better train the AI algorithms, once they are trained AI algorithms can predict in astounding perfection when only a small data is available. Here chances are prominent that only a handful of IT giants, who own and collect a massive amount of data every day will monopolize the benefits of the AI technology, since even the most sophisticated AI algorithm needs high-quality, high-volume data to be able to generalize to new situations. Recently, major IT companies are publicly declaring their will to democratize AI, making it for every person and every organization.

However, in order for everyone to have access to AI technologies that pay incredible dividends for companies like Google and Facebook, lesser players in the field must also have access to the volume of data that are available for the big players—which they do not, because, data, an increasingly important asset is zealously kept private by the big companies. At this stage of development AI democratization can hardly sound realistic, if we do not democratize data first.

Oxford University author Nick Bostrom in his pioneering book "Superintelligence: Paths, Dangers, Strategies" talks at length about the risk of a monopolized or secretive AI development and its negative impact on society as the risk of "technological singularity".

However, with the help of block chain technology, democratization of AI technology seems somewhat possible. Its core ideas, democratic by design, have inspired many new AI democratization initiatives. With block chain technology, which essentially enables the creation of always growing, robust, collective and distributed datasets without the need of trusted third-party with privileged access to them, democratization of AI will be much easier. The availability of huge distributed data will help the analysis, prediction and assessment of new algorithms.

The smart use of Blockchain technologies – not storing data itself on it, but meta-data – can enforce availability and integrity that serve as verifiable service agreements without the need of a trusted third-party. A group of blockchain-based AI initiatives like OpenMined, SingularityNet, and ConsensusAI share this idea. Even if at their early-stage of development, the potential of these projects looks incredibly high due to their ability to create data commons without intermediation. An open marketplace for data, algorithms and computation, would surely help even small companies and organizations to catch up with state-of-the-art AI systems.

Human Machine Co-evolution

Any AI system that co-exists with people as part of their daily lives must be able to learn and adapt to new experiences. As designers, we simply cannot envisage all the possible scenarios that such a systems will encounter. The challenge is not only to build an AI system that is an active learner, but to build an AI system that can serve and love humanity in a way that is natural and intuitive.

In CAI, the interaction between human and machine will be like evolutionary interactions between flowering plants and bees. Development of compassionate AI system is a gradual process. As discussed earlier the compassionate AI systems can be classified into three groups. They are: Narrow Compassionate AI, General Compassionate AI and Compassionate

Superintelligence. Narrow Compassionate AI tries to remove pains at individual level. General Compassionate AI tries to remove pains at social level, group level or country level. Compassionate Superintelligence tries to remove pains at higher levels of humanity.

Scientists all over the world increasingly feel that consciousness can be digitized and can be implemented in machine. Initially, it was thought absurd. But with compassion-driven deep learning algorithms, such as the RDC algorithms, it looks much feasible.

Human and AI systems will be deeply connected through value networks without an evident leader or strong hierarchical structures. The whole system will run on the basis of shared responsibility. The network may not be always visible, and it will exist as a distributed system. Neither the machine nor the humans will be subordinate to anyone. Both will work and thrive together and will cooperate with each other. As the source knowledge will be distributed, the network will run on the basis of mutual trust, benevolence, welfare and compassion.

Conclusion

In this book, we have discussed the goal, scope, principles, framework and algorithms for the development of compassionate artificial intelligence. We have also discussed the computational aspect of compassion. We have introduced six indexes of consciousness and also the RDC algorithms for compassionate AI. We have discussed eleven key characteristics, five design principles and twelve behavior principles of compassionate AI agents. We have explored the possibilities of cellular programming and genetic editing for evolving compassion and deep-intelligence. We have also discussed the need for joint evolution and empowerment of humans and machines for the betterment of society.

Unless machines and human co-evolve, there is the impending risk that machines will surpass human intelligence in every aspect, and they may treat humans like pets or inferior beings with lower intelligence and compassion compared to them. Then the human liberty, and dignity will be at risk, and humans might be the victims of the systems designed by themselves.

We have discussed the possible means of coevolution of humans and machines by introducing RDC compassion algorithms, so that AI systems work in associations of the humans — and not against them — for the betterment of the society and the planet. Compassionate collective human-machine joint intelligence will be a boon to the future human society.

A good AI requires a computational framework that is constantly learning, constantly adaptive and constantly benevolent. We hope compassionate AI will eliminate the pain and suffering from the society and will bring more happiness and joy. Compassionate AI is our commitment to the next generations for freedom, love and caring. Compassionate AI is the blueprint to allow the humans to sing the song of their hearts.

In summary, we provided a wide-angled lens overview of what this new field is, suggested how to propel the field forward, and provided a vision for the near future, with "compassionate artificial intelligence" representing a paradigm shift that promises to change the landscape of how AI is currently conceived.

A humbling reminder that we still have much work to do in order to get meaningful progress in the field of compassionate AI. In the coming years, the true test of whether we could deliver on the promise of CAI will require us to prospectively define clear and meaningful end points, develop a clear strategy, and then demonstrate that we can achieve them. A clear strategy is required to ensure that the society as a whole will benefit from the evolution of AI and its potential adverse effects are removed from early stages, by using the concept of "compassion by design" and "safety by design". Such fears should not hinder the progress of AI but motivate the development of a systematic framework on which the future AI will flourish.

References

Ahn, W.-Y., Rass, O., Shin, Y.-W., Busemeyer, J. R., Brown, J. W., & O'Donnell, B. F. (2012). Emotion-based reinforcement learning. *Proceedings of the 34th Annual Conference of the Cognitive Science Society*, *1*, 78–83. Retrieved from http://mindmodeling.org/cogsci2012/papers/0027/paper0027.pdf

Beaty, R., Benedek, M., Silvia, P., Sciences, D. S.-T. in cognitive, & 2016, U. (2016). Creative cognition and brain network dynamics. *Trends in Cognitive Sciences*, *20*(2), 87–95. Retrieved from https://www.sciencedirect.com/science/article/pii/S1364661315002545

Boden, M. A. (1992). *The Creative Mind. . Abacus, London.* https://doi.org/10.1080/07421656.2004.10129694

Bostrom, N. (2014). Superintelligence: Paths, dangers, strategies. *Superintelligence: Paths, Dangers, Strategies.* https://doi.org/10.1017/S0031819115000340

Brundage, M., Avin, S., Clark, J., Allen, G. C., Flynn, C., Farquhar, S., … Bryson, J. (2018). *The Malicious Use of Artificial Intelligence: Forecasting, Prevention and Mitigation.* University of Oxford. Retrieved from https://maliciousaireport.com

Colton, S., & Wiggins, G. A. (2012). Computational creativity: The final frontier? *Frontiers in Artificial Intelligence and Applications*, *242*, 21–26. https://doi.org/10.3233/978-1-61499-098-7-21

Damasio, A., & Carvalho, G. B. (2013). The nature of feelings: Evolutionary and neurobiological origins. *Nature Reviews Neuroscience*, *14*(2), 143–152. https://doi.org/10.1038/nrn3403

Del R. Millán, J., & Carmena, J. M. (2010). Invasive or

noninvasive: Understanding brain-machine interface technology. *IEEE Engineering in Medicine and Biology Magazine*, *29*(1), 16–22. https://doi.org/10.1109/MEMB.2009.935475

Doyon, J., Bellec, P., Amsel, R., Penhune, V., Monchi, O., Carrier, J., … Benali, H. (2009). Contributions of the basal ganglia and functionally related brain structures to motor learning. *Behavioural Brain Research*, *199*(1), 61–75. https://doi.org/10.1016/j.bbr.2008.11.012

Eisenbeiss, H. (2011). The Potential of Unmanned Aerial Vehicles for Mapping. *Photogrammetrische Woche 2011*, 135–145.

Foerster, J. N., Assael, Y. M., de Freitas, N., & Whiteson, S. (2016). Learning to Communicate with Deep Multi-Agent Reinforcement Learning. *Technical Report ArXiv:1602.02672,*. https://doi.org/10.7551/ecal

Fösel, T., Tighineanu, P., Weiss, T., & Marquardt, F. (2018). Reinforcement Learning with Neural Networks for Quantum Feedback. Retrieved from http://arxiv.org/abs/1802.05267

Friston, K. (2010). The free-energy principle: A unified brain theory? *Nature Reviews Neuroscience*, *11*(2), 127–138. https://doi.org/10.1038/nrn2787

Goetz, J., Keltner, D., & Simon-Thomas, E. (2010). Compassion: An Evolutionary Analysis and Empirical Review. *Psychol Bull*, *136*(3), 351–374. Retrieved from http://ovidsp.ovid.com/ovidweb.cgi?T=JS&PAGE=reference&D=paovftk&NEWS=N&AN=00006823-201005000-00006

Good, I. J. (1965). Speculations Concerning the First Ultraintelligent Machine. *Advances in Computers*, 31–88. https://doi.org/10.1016/S0065-2458(08)60418-0

Gottfredson, L. S. (1997). Mainstream science on intelligence: An editorial with 52 signatories, history, and bibliography. *Intelligence*, *24*(1), 13–23. https://doi.org/10.1016/S0160-2896(97)90011-8

Guliford JP. (1967). the Nature of Human Intelligence. *The Nature of HUman Intelligence*, 538–539.

Hausknecht, M., & Stone, P. (2015). Deep Recurrent Q-Learning for Partially Observable MDPs. *Technical Report ArXiv: 1507.06527V4*. https://doi.org/10.1.1.696.1421

Kanov, J. M., Maitlis, S., Worline, M. C., Dutton, J. E., Frost, P. J., & Lilius, J. M. (2004). Compassion in Organizational Life. *American Behavioral Scientist*, *47*(6), 808–827. https://doi.org/10.1177/0002764203260211

Keramati, M., & Gutkin, B. (2014). Homeostatic reinforcement learning for integrating reward collection and physiological stability. *ELife*, *3*. https://doi.org/10.7554/eLife.04811

Kirby, J., Doty, J. M., Petrocchi, N., & Gilbert, P. (2017). The Current and Future Role of Heart Rate Variability for Assessing and Training Compassion. *Frontiers in Public Health*, *5*(March), 40. https://doi.org/10.3389/FPUBH.2017.00040

Kok, B. E., & Fredrickson, B. L. (2010). Upward spirals of the heart: Autonomic flexibility, as indexed by vagal tone, reciprocally and prospectively predicts positive emotions and social connectedness. *Biological Psychology*, *85*(3), 432–436. https://doi.org/10.1016/j.biopsycho.2010.09.005

Liu, C. Y., Chen, C., Chang, C. Ter, & Shih, L. M. (2013). Single-hidden-layer feed-forward quantum neural network based on Grover learning. *Neural Networks*, *45*, 144–150. https://doi.org/10.1016/j.neunet.2013.02.012

Longe, O., Maratos, F. A., Gilbert, P., Evans, G., Volker, F., Rockliff, H., & Rippon, G. (2010). Having a word with yourself: Neural correlates of self-criticism and self-reassurance. *NeuroImage*, *49*(2), 1849–1856. https://doi.org/10.1016/j.neuroimage.2009.09.019

Lutz, A., Brefczynski-Lewis, J., Johnstone, T., & Davidson, R. J. (2008). Regulation of the neural circuitry of emotion by compassion meditation: Effects of meditative expertise. *PLoS ONE*, *3*(3).

https://doi.org/10.1371/journal.pone.0001897

Marinier, R. P., Laird, J. E., & Marinier Iii, R. P. (2008). Emotion-Driven Reinforcement Learning. *Proceedings of the 30th Annual Conference of the Cognitive Science Society*, 115–120.

Mnih, V., Badia, A. P., Mirza, M., Graves, A., Lillicrap, T. P., Harley, T., … Kavukcuoglu, K. (2016). Asynchronous Methods for Deep Reinforcement Learning. https://doi.org/10.1177/0956797613514093

Mnih, V., Kavukcuoglu, K., Silver, D., Rusu, A. A., Veness, J., Bellemare, M. G., … Petersen, S. (2015). Human-level control through deep reinforcement learning. *Nature*, *518*(7540), 529–533.

Nordrum, A. (2016). Popular Internet of Things Forecast of 50 Billion Devices by 2020 Is Outdated. *IEEE Spectrum*, 0–2. Retrieved from https://spectrum.ieee.org/tech-talk/telecom/internet/popular-internet-of-things-forecast-of-50-billion-devices-by-2020-is-outdated

Nussbaum, M. (1996). Compassion: The Basic Social Emotion. *Social Philosophy and Policy*, *13*(01), 27. https://doi.org/10.1017/S0265052500001515

Patel, K. K., & Patel, S. M. (2016). Internet of Things-IOT: definition, characteristics, architecture, enabling technologies, application & future challenges. *International Journal of Engineering Science and Computing*, *6*(5), 6122–6131. https://doi.org/10.4010/2016.1482

Pavuluri, M., & May, A. (2015). I Feel, Therefore, I am: The Insula and Its Role in Human Emotion, Cognition and the Sensory-Motor System. *AIMS Neuroscience*, *2*(1), 18–27.

Pétervári, J., Osman, M., & Bhattacharya, J. (2016). The role of intuition in the generation and evaluation stages of creativity. *Frontiers in Psychology*, *7*(SEP). https://doi.org/10.3389/fpsyg.2016.01420

Poniszewska-Maranda, A., & Kaczmarek, D. (2015). Selected

methods of artificial intelligence for Internet of Things conception. *Conference on Computer Science and Information Systems*, 1343–1348. https://doi.org/10.15439/2015F161

Porges, S. W. (2009). The polyvagal theory: New insights into adaptive reactions of the autonomic nervous system. *Cleveland Clinic Journal of Medicine*, *76*(SUPPL.2). https://doi.org/10.3949/ccjm.76.s2.17

Rameson, L. T., Morelli, S. A., & Lieberman, M. D. (2012). The Neural Correlates of Empathy: Experience, Automaticity, and Prosocial Behavior. *Journal of Cognitive Neuroscience*, *24*(1), 235–245. https://doi.org/10.1162/jocn_a_00130

Ray, A. K. (1991). Equipment fault diagnosis - A neural network approach. *Computers in Industry*, *16*, 169–177.

Ray, A. K., & Bhattacharyya, D. . (1994). Stepless PWM speed control of AC motors : A neural network approach. *Neurocomputing*, *6*, 523–539.

Ray, A. K., & Misra, R. B. (1992). Real-time fault diagnosis - using occupancy grids and neural network techniques. *Lecture Notes in Computer Science (Including Subseries Lecture Notes in Artificial Intelligence and Lecture Notes in Bioinformatics), Vol. 604 Springer, Berlin, Heidelberg, 604 LNAI.*

Reber, P. (2010). What Is the Memory Capacity of the Human Brain? *Scientific American*. Retrieved from http://www.scientificamerican.com/article.cfm?id=what-is-the-memory-capacity

Russell, Stuart J.; Norvig, P. (2003). *Artificial Intelligence: A Modern Approach*. Prentice Hall.

Russell, S., & Norvig, P. (2010). Artificial Intelligence: A Modern Approach.

Silver, D., Schrittwieser, J., Simonyan, K., Antonoglou, I., Huang, A., Guez, A., … Hassabis, D. (2017). Mastering the game of Go without human knowledge. *Nature*, *550*(7676), 354–359.

https://doi.org/10.1038/nature24270

Statt, N. (2018). Skydio's AI-powered autonomous R1 drone follows you around in 4K. *The Verge*. Retrieved from https://www.theverge.com/2018/2/13/17006010/skydio-r1-autonomous-drone-4k-video-recording-ai-computer-vision-mapping

Stellar, J. E., Cohen, A., Oveis, C., & Keltner, D. (2015). Affective and physiological responses to the suffering of others: Compassion and vagal activity. *Journal of Personality and Social Psychology*, *108*(4), 572–585. https://doi.org/10.1037/pspi0000010

Strauss, C., Lever Taylor, B., Gu, J., Kuyken, W., Baer, R., Jones, F., & Cavanagh, K. (2016). What is compassion and how can we measure it? A review of definitions and measures. *Clinical Psychology Review*, *47*, 15–27. https://doi.org/10.1016/j.cpr.2016.05.004

Sutton, R. S., & Barto, A. (1998). *Reinforcement learning: An introduction*. Cambridge: MIT Press.

Turing, A. M. (1950). Computing machinery and intelligence. *Mind*. https://doi.org/10.1007/978-1-4020-6710-5_3

Wan, K. H., Dahlsten, O., Kristjánsson, H., Gardner, R., & Kim, M. S. (2016). Quantum generalisation of feedforward neural networks. *Technical Report ArXiv: 1612.01045*. https://doi.org/10.1038/s41534-017-0032-4

Watkins, C. J. C. H., & Dayan, P. (1992). Q-learning. In *Machine Learning* (p. 8:279–292).

Y. LeCun Y. Bengio, & Hinton, G. (2015). Deep learning. *Nature*. https://doi.org/10.1038/nature14539

Zhang, J., Cheng, W., Liu, Z., Zhang, K., Lei, X., Yao, Y., … Feng, J. (2016). Neural, electrophysiological and anatomical basis of brain-network variability and its characteristic changes in mental disorders. *Brain*, *139*(8), 2307–2321. https://doi.org/10.1093/brain/aww143

Zhu, P., Li, X., Poupart, P., & Miao, G. (2017). On Improving Deep Reinforcement Learning for POMDPs. *Technical Report ArXiv: 1704.0797*. Retrieved from http://arxiv.org/abs/1704.07978

About the Author

Dr. Amit Ray is an AI scientist of international repute and a spiritual master of meditation and compassion. He has implemented many large scale AI projects across the world. He has published several articles on artificial intelligence and neuro-computing in international journals and conferences. He did his PhD in artificial intelligence and computational neuroscience and worked as scientist in India, USA and UK. He is author of several books on meditation and science. He is the founder of compassionate artificial intelligence lab.

Made in the USA
Monee, IL
22 July 2025

21701884R00152